THE MOST IMPORTANT *Women* OF THE BIBLE

THE MOST IMPORTANT *Women* OF THE BIBLE

Remarkable Stories of God's Love and Redemption

AARON AND ELAINA SHARP

BETHANYHOUSE
a division of Baker Publishing Group
Minneapolis, Minnesota

Published by Bethany House Publishers
11400 Hampshire Avenue South
Bloomington, Minnesota 55438
www.bethanyhouse.com

Bethany House Publishers is a division of
Baker Publishing Group, Grand Rapids, Michigan

Printed in the United States of America

ISBN 978-0-7642-1962-7

Library of Congress Control Number: 2017945993

Cover design by Rob Williams, InsideOutCreativeArts

18 19 20 21 22 23 7 6 5 4 3 2

In keeping with biblical principles of creation stewardship, Baker Publishing Group advocates the responsible use of our natural resources. As a member of the Green Press Initiative, our company uses recycled paper when possible. The text paper of this book is composed in part of post-consumer waste.

Contents

Introduction

This book is all about the women of the Bible and the role they played in God's plan of redemption for humanity. This book is also coauthored by a husband and wife. Knowing this, it might come as a surprise to you that in a book about biblical women, coauthored by a woman with a master's degree in theology, a man wrote the Introduction.

Far too often when we talk about the role of women in the church, gender in general, or frankly any topic, everything seems to boil down to one word—*power.* Who has the power? Who wants the power? Who is being kept powerless? How do we speak truth to power? These questions seem to percolate at or just below the surface of a great number of issues today, particularly when the topic has anything to do with the sexes.

Over the course of my life, I have been blessed to be raised by, influenced by, married to, and friends with an extraordinary number of godly women. None of these women were perfect (though my coauthor certainly comes close), but there is one thing they all have in common—a focus on eternity.

Truth be told, I doubt that any of these women would have thought to describe themselves as eternally focused, but as an observer I can tell you that the depiction is a true one. Even now, often years or even decades after the fact, the impressions left on me are unforgettable.

In my mind there is the image of a grandmother who never had much in the way of material possessions; whose husband succumbed frequently to temptations of adultery, alcohol abuse, and myriad other vices; who never stopped going to church; who never stopped praying for every single member of her family; who took what little money she had for a weekly hair appointment and gave it to the church's mission offering. Would that little lady have thought of herself as eternally focused? No doubt the husband, whose residence in heaven today is largely due to her prayers, would say so. When I think about it, I can picture the confused look on her face had anyone ever asked her if she was focused on eternity, but I can tell you as one of the many whom she loved and influenced that she most certainly was.

There is another image in my mind. This one is also of a grandmother. In many ways the two grandmothers' stories are similar. This one also prayed persistently until a husband accepted Christ, albeit at a much earlier period in life. Her love for God's Word practically radiated from her skin—she devoured new commentaries and was quick to pose theological questions to a seminarian grandson, even if some of them revolved around the eternal state of her beloved and long-since-departed dog. Today, there are men and women nearing retirement age who speak glowingly of the Sunday school lessons she taught when they were small children. Maybe she would never have used the phrase *eternally focused* in reference to herself, but that makes it no less an accurate description.

I could go on and on, but my mother will read this book expecting not to be a part of this Introduction (deserving though she may be), and my wife will coauthor the rest of this book, no doubt removing anything I might write about her. These women who have made an impact on my life are merely the latest in a long line of women of faith who lived their lives for eternity. In the Bible we see an abundance of women who had a part to play in God's plan of redemption.

To twenty-first-century Christians, the women of the Bible can easily become two-dimensional characters in the black-and-white print of an old book. We must remember three facts about the life and times of the women who grace the Bible's pages. First, thanks to the sin of Adam and Eve in the garden of Eden, all of humanity was in desperate need of redemption. This need left every human being on planet Earth hopeless. Sin was a spiritual disease that humanity was unable to remedy by itself. Second, Jesus, through His death, burial, and resurrection brought about redemption. Where humanity was incapable of doing anything about its sin problem, God himself provided the answer in the person of His Son. Third, what we have today in the written Word of God is the story of redemption for humanity brought about by God. This redemption is promised by God at the beginning of Genesis, finds its culmination in the life of Jesus in the Gospels, and is proclaimed throughout the rest of the New Testament. The life of every man, woman, and child in the Bible either looks forward to the coming of redemption by Jesus, or it looks backward to the work of redemption that has already been done by Christ.

In that respect, just about every person in the Scriptures could be described as a participant in God's redemptive plan. Every person in the Bible is another brushstroke in the beautiful painting of redemption that God painted. Rather than looking at every single brushstroke in the painting, however, this book will focus primarily on the women God used to further His plan. It is impossible to tell the story of redemption without telling the story of women.

This book is not an exhaustive look at the women of the Bible, and some notable women were left out. Our look at the women who played a role in God's redemptive plan will begin where you might expect—in the garden of Eden. From there it will take us through Israel, Egypt, Greece, and various other locations. We will see sisters, wives, mothers, widows, queens, slaves, prostitutes, businesswomen, grandmothers, and a mother-in-law. What every one of these women has in common has a very important part to play in God's plan to redeem the human race, and to bring to himself a group of people that He would call His own. This is their story.

1

Eve

The First Woman, the First Sinner

Should God create another Eve, and I
Another Rib afford, yet loss of thee
Would never from my heart; no, no, I feel
The Link of Nature draw me: Flesh of Flesh,
Bone of my Bone thou art, and from thy State
Mine never shall be parted, bliss or woe.[1]

—John Milton, *Paradise Lost*

Scripture References

Genesis 2, 3, 4; 2 Corinthians 11; 1 Timothy 2

Biography

There is not a lot of agreement about when the first woman's beginning took place. The book of Genesis is not entirely clear as to whether she was created with Adam on the sixth day of creation, or if God's special act of creating the first woman came after day seven. Good people disagree as to the timing, but one thing that is definitely clear is that the first woman's creation was unique.

God observed how the man living in the garden of Eden was alone, and His solution to this issue was to create a companion for Adam that would fit perfectly with him. Genesis 2:18 says, "I will make him a helper suitable for him" (NASB). Many English Bibles use the word *suitable* to translate the Hebrew word *kÿnegdo*, which means "opposite to" or "corresponding to." The idea behind the creation of woman was that God would create a mate that matched the man in the garden in a way that completed him. It was as if they were two pieces of a puzzle that fit together perfectly.

God's method of creating a companion for Adam was to put him into a deep sleep, and then to remove a rib, which God then used to form Adam's companion. This act caused the first act of a smitten man writing a poem in honor of his soul mate. Adam declared, "This is now bone of my bones, and flesh of my flesh; she shall be called Woman, because she was taken out of Man" (Genesis 2:23 NASB). The only two human beings on the planet were naked, unashamed, and "one flesh." The happy couple lived peacefully in communion with God and animals. The only thing they had to do was not to eat of one tree in the middle of the garden.

Of course, all would not remain perfect in the idyllic garden. A walking, talking serpent convinced the woman that just maybe God had lied, or was not serious about the one rule He had given them. She bought the snake's lies, ate the fruit, gave her husband a bite, and humanity capsized into the depths of sin. When confronted by God, Adam blamed his wife, and she in turn pointed her finger at the serpent's deception. God responded by proclaiming curses on the snake and the world's first couple. For her part, God told the woman, "I will greatly multiply your pain in childbirth, in pain you will bring forth children; yet your desire will be for your husband, and he will rule over you" (Genesis 3:16 NASB).

God made clothes for the couple out of animal skins to cover their nakedness, and it was at this point that Adam gave his wife the name *Eve* because she was going to be "the mother of all the living" (v. 20). Because of their now sinful natures, God drove Adam and Eve from the garden, never to return again.

Role in Redemption

For obvious reasons, Eve has never been the most popular biblical role model for women. Unfortunately for Eve, we don't know much about her, and what we do know is not good. Aside from being deceived by the serpent and committing sin, all we know is that she gave birth to three sons, the eldest of which murdered the middle brother in cold blood. Not exactly the legacy that most women are looking to leave.

Eve's reputation probably isn't helped any by the fact that the rest of the Scriptures have precious little to say about her. After naming her third son *Seth* at the end of Genesis 4, Eve passes from the scene and is never mentioned again throughout the entire Old Testament. She only gets two brief mentions in the New Testament, both of which are by the apostle Paul referencing her deception in the garden. In 2 Corinthians 11:3, Paul warns the believers in Corinth by saying, "But I am afraid that, as the serpent deceived Eve by his craftiness, your minds will be led astray from the simplicity and purity of devotion to Christ" (NASB). Then in 1 Timothy 2:13–14, while giving Timothy instructions about gender roles in church, he says, "For it was Adam who was first created, and then Eve. And it was not

Adam who was deceived, but the woman being deceived, fell into transgression" (NASB).

A cursory glance of what the Scriptures say, and do not say, might lead us to the conclusion that the only role Eve played in God's plan of redemption was being part of the problem. A deeper look, however, gives us a glimpse of a bigger role that she played.

After their sin, God pronounced judgment on Adam, Eve, and the serpent. First, He addressed the snake, then Eve. God's final words to the serpent included words that applied to Eve as well: "I will put enmity between you and the woman, and between your seed and her seed; he shall bruise you on the head, and you shall bruise him on the heel" (Genesis 3:15 NASB).

This passage is very noteworthy for a number of reasons. First, this is the initial promise of a redeemer. The Old Testament contains hundreds of prophecies of a coming Messiah, and right here, in the garden, in the aftermath of humanity's fall into sin, is the first promise that God has a plan to redeem mankind. Second, this passage is striking because of who it is addressed to. In Genesis 3:15, God is still speaking to the serpent, but His words to the snake involve and have bearing on Eve as well.

In the New Testament, Eve is said to have been deceived by the serpent, but the responsibility for sin entering the world is laid at the feet of Adam, not Eve. Romans 5:12 says, "Therefore, just as through one man sin entered into the world, and death through sin, and so death spread to all men, because all sinned" (NASB). Also, 1 Corinthians 15:22 tells us, "For as in Adam all die, so also in Christ all will be made alive" (NASB).

Adam's culpability in the eyes of God is what makes the first promise of a Savior all the more telling. God's promise was not that there would be enmity between the man and the serpent, but between the woman and the serpent. It would be the seed of the serpent and the seed of the woman—not the man—that would continue in hostility. Even though God would ultimately hold Adam responsible for what happened in the garden, this promise is specifically focused on the woman's role in bringing about redemption, which would now be necessary because of Eve's actions.

Eve's reputation as the woman who ate the fruit and plunged the world into sin is not untrue, but it is not the whole truth. Where the serpent brought forth deception God brought forth truth. Where the serpent sought to bring about destruction God promised to bring healing. Where the serpent brought death God vowed to bring life.

The snake intended his deception of Eve to be the downfall of humanity, and the ruin of Eve. From God's perspective, however, the exact opposite would ultimately be true. God's promise was from His perspective: Eve would not be remembered for *what she did*. No, God would act, and in so doing Eve would be remembered for *what God would do*.

God did not promise to give Eve or her offspring a second chance. He did not respond by asking or demanding that Eve somehow redeem herself, or by giving her a pathway to work her way back into His good graces. The first promise of a Savior, delivered to a devious serpent, about the woman's place in God's plan was solely and exclusively about what God would do for Eve.

From that point on, Eve, her husband, and all of their offspring would exist in a world where sin ran rampant. The faults of the first couple would exist and multiply in every generation that would come after them. Yet, in this darkest of moments, God's promise shines forth as a beacon. Eve was not just the woman who sinned in eating the fruit; she was the recipient of God's first promise of the coming of a Savior.

By the Numbers

Bible verses that mention Eve by name: 4

Bible books in which she is mentioned: 3

Women on the earth before Eve: 0

Talking snakes encountered by Eve: 1

Things We Wondered

What did Adam and Eve use to sew fig leaves together?

How many children did Eve actually give birth to?

2

Sarah

The Laugher

> Sarah's acceptance of a promise which at first she seemed to hear with indifference is . . . a venture into the unseen world which faith makes real.[1]
>
> —F. F. Bruce

Scripture References

Genesis 11, 12, 16, 17, 18, 21, 23, 24, 25, 49; Isaiah 51; Romans 4, 9; Galatians 4; Hebrews 11; 1 Peter 2

Biography

Sarah actually made her debut in Scripture with the name *Sarai*. It may seem strange in today's culture, but she married her half-brother Abram, who is one of the great patriarchs of the Old Testament.

There is no specific time line given; the Bible tells of Abram and Sarai as a married couple leaving their homeland of Ur with their father and other family members. The group's intention was to travel to the land of Canaan, but they stopped and settled in Haran before they finished their journey.

When God appeared before Abram in Genesis 12, He instructed him to leave his homeland and his family and go "to the land which I will show you." Abram does obey God by leaving his homeland, but he does not leave his family behind. His nephew Lot went with Abram and Sarai, and we discover later that this causes conflict among the family because of land disputes.

God also gave a promise to Abram, saying, "And I will make of you a great nation, and I will bless you and make your name great, so that you will be a blessing. I will bless those who bless you and him who dishonors you I will curse, and in you all the families of the earth shall be blessed" (Genesis 12:1–3). As Abram's wife, God included Sarah in this promise, intending that she be the mother of Abram's descendants. She, too, forsook her family and homeland to follow God.

After they had settled in Canaan for a period of time, a famine struck the land and forced Abram to take his family to Egypt to escape its severity. Now, Abram knew that Sarai was beautiful, and guessing that the Egyptians might kill him in order to claim Sarai as their own, Abram feared for his life. He convinced Sarai to follow his lead and to tell the Egyptians that they were merely brother and sister, which omitted the truth of their marriage. Pharaoh and his princes praised Sarai for her beauty, and took her into Pharaoh's house. God ultimately intervened and sent great plagues upon the Egyptians until they released Sarai back to Abram. This was the first time that Abram and Sarai lied about their relationship.

A decade passed, and Sarai became tired of waiting for God to open her womb. She was impatient and decided to follow her own wisdom rather than God's wisdom, so she gave her handmaiden Hagar to Abram, supposing that the best way for her to obtain children was through her maid. Abram went along with Sarai's plan, and Hagar gave birth to a son named Ishmael. The outcome of this, which can only be described as utterly predictable, was that a significant strain emerged between the two women, with Abram stuck in the middle. In a strange way, there is symmetry in the plans that Abram and Sarai cooked up to "help" each other. Abram lied about their marriage, Sarai gave him her handmaid to produce an heir, and neither followed God.

Genesis 17 describes another encounter whereby God changed Abram's name to Abraham and Sarai's name to Sarah. The change in names signified God's renewed promise to make Abraham into a great nation, and included Sarah because it would be her child—not Hagar's child—through whom this promise would be fulfilled. God's intentions for Sarah were clear: "I will bless her, and she shall be a mother of nations; kings of peoples will come from her" (Genesis 17:16 NASB).

The Lord again appeared to Abraham in Genesis 18, where He gave specific details as to when the promise of a child would be fulfilled. God said that He would return around the same time the next year, and that Abraham and Sarah would have a son. Suffice it to say that when Sarah overheard Abraham's conversation with the Lord she was a bit skeptical. Indeed, her initial response was to laugh at the absurdity of expecting a child at her advanced age, but her mirth soon gave way to fear. God heard her laugh and knew the disbelief she harbored in her heart.

The second instance of Abraham and Sarah being less than truthful about their marital relationship happened in Genesis 20, when Abraham traveled with his family to Gerar. The passage does not give an explanation for their travel, but as before,

Sarah went along with Abraham's plan and did not tell the entire truth to King Abimelech. Even at her "advanced age," King Abimelech desired Sarah and sent for her. Once again, God intervened. He revealed the truth to Abimelech through a dream before he sinned by touching Sarah. It is clear that Sarah was sheltered under God's protection and was part of His plan for the nation of Israel.

After their brief side trip to Gerar, the long-awaited promise of a child was fulfilled! Sarah had waited decades to see the fruit of her womb, and finally she gave birth to Isaac, whose name means "laughter." Sarah seems to have found some sort of sense of humor at this point, for she says, "God has made laughter for me; everyone who hears will laugh with me. . . . Who would have said to Abraham that Sarah would nurse children? Yet I have borne him a son in his old age" (Genesis 21:6–7 NASB).

Once again, tensions between Sarah and Hagar intensified because of jealousy, hurt, and anger. This struggle culminated in Abraham's sending Hagar and Ishmael away at the behest of Sarah, but God intervened on their behalf and protected them and provided for them. God never wavered on His promise to fulfill Abraham's legacy through Sarah, but He also provided for Hagar and Ishmael in their desperation, being cast off because they were linked to Abraham.

Although Sarah was never mentioned in Genesis 22, this passage is significant and necessary to include in her biography. After so many decades of waiting for a son, God tests Abraham and instructs him to sacrifice Isaac. Abraham was devoted to the Lord, and obeyed God's instructions without question. He begins preparations to give up his son, through whom God's promises of making Abraham a great nation were to be fulfilled. It is only when Abraham lifts up his knife and is about to slaughter Isaac that God stays his hand. He says, "Do not lay your hand on the boy or do anything to him, for now I know that you fear God, seeing you have not withheld your son, your only son, from me" (Genesis 22:12). God himself provides another sacrifice in the form of a ram, and so spares the life of Isaac. There is no biblical record of Sarah's feelings or reactions to this unconventional command of God to Abraham, but one can only imagine the grief and confusion she must have been feeling.

Though the text is not clear, and biblical historians are unsure, it is at least possible that Abraham and Sarah were living in different locations after the events of Genesis 22. Sarah's life ended at the age of 127, and Abraham buried her in the cave of the field at Machpelah facing Mamre, in the land of Canaan.

Role in Redemption

The easiest thing to do with biblical characters is to treat them as two-dimensional figures, to think of them as letters on a page rather than to remember that they were real people. Real people get angry, make bad decisions, and get up on the wrong side of the bed. If reading about someone in the Bible doesn't make you ask the question "What must that have felt like?" you are missing a very important piece of the puzzle.

Sarah, who is first introduced as Sarai, is a prime example of the necessity of trying to see the world through the eyes of the person who lived it. What did it feel like to be married to a man who lied about being married to you—twice? What did it feel like to wait endlessly for God's promise to be fulfilled? What was it like to urge your husband to make the wrong decision, and to feel the pain of that mistake for years? How much pressure was there to fix a meal for visitors, when one of them was God? Some of these questions are certainly unique to Sarah, but the matriarch's contribution to God's plan of redemption has implications for the entire community of faith.

First, God's interactions with Sarah show clearly that, in the eyes of God, doubt is not a terminal disease. Many people might think doubt would eliminate Sarah from being part of God's plan. As theologian C. Michael Patton expresses it,

> There are so many Christians out there who will not understand [doubt] because they have been taught for so long to immediately shove their doubts in a closet in the back of their mind. Therefore, they are probably in denial about them. As well, they may look down upon you for having doubts and/or question your salvation.[2]

Denying doubt might be a common reaction, but Sarah's doubts did not preclude her from being part of God's plans. God's words to Sarah and Abraham caused her to try to bring about the fulfillment of the promises through her own methods, to laugh at the impossibility of the situation, and to lie about laughing at God's promises. Despite all of this, God's choice of Sarah as the mother of nations proved to be unshakable.

Second, not only were Sarah's doubts not terminal, but through humor and irony those doubts gave birth to hope. Initially, Abraham laughed at the idea of becoming a father in his old age (Genesis 17:17), then Sarah laughed at the thought of birthing a child in her ninth decade of life (Genesis 18:12). When God asked Sarah why she laughed—whether through fear, embarrassment, or some other motivation—she lied about it. One might expect that a year later, when these past-their-prime parents held their newborn son in their arms, their previous doubts would have been the farthest from their minds. Instead, Sarah's only child was named Isaac, which means "laughter." Though the book of Genesis does not tell us whether Isaac was named by his father or his mother, Sarah says something in Genesis 21, which may indicate that the name was her idea, or at the very least shows that she was on board with the name. After giving birth to a new son, Sarah was once again laughing, but now her laughter was different. In Genesis 21:6, she says, "God has made laughter for me; everyone who hears will laugh with me" (NASB). Where there had once been the laughter of doubt, there was now the laughter of joy. There are few things more indicative of God's redemptive power than taking a symbol of pain and turning it into a symbol of joy.

Third, the New Testament presents Sarah as an example of faith for all believers and for wives in particular. In Hebrews 11:11, Sarah is commended for having faith in a faithful God. In 1 Peter 3:6, her willful deference to her husband is held up as a model for wives who might be enduring mistreatment or difficult times. One commentator, when describing the overall message of the book of 1 Peter, said,

> The behavior of believers when they encounter unfair circumstances should reflect a spirit of deference in all relationships as they follow Christ's example and anticipate future glory.[3]

Think of that: the last biblical reference to Sarah is when her story is featured prominently in 1 Peter, a book centered on being eternally focused by following Christ in trying situations.

It would be easy to look at Sarah and to assume that her contribution to God's plan to redeem mankind was limited to giving birth to the child who fulfilled God's promise. Being the mother of Isaac meant that Sarah would be the mother of the nation of Israel. The Messiah that would emerge from that nation would be her descendant. God used Sarah, even in her old age, to give life to His promises. Her role as a mother was tremendous, but her contribution includes so much more.

By the Numbers

Children to whom Sarah gave birth: 1

Age at which Sarah gave birth to Isaac: 90

Age at which Sarah decided she was "too old for this": 90

Age at which Sarah died: 127

Things We Wondered

Why did Sarai and her family settle in Haran instead of finishing their journey to Canaan in Genesis 11? Why did they leave Ur in the first place?

Were Abraham and Sarah separated, or at least living separately, when she died?

Did Sarah know of God's command that Abraham sacrifice Isaac? What were her reactions if she did know?

3

Tamar

The Jilted Daughter-in-Law

> In this story, Tamar is His unlikely tool. She is a Canaanite, a daughter of the very people against whom Abraham had warned and whom the children of Israel would later displace. Tamar is treated with respect; her desperate deed draws no condemnation from the Torah. What she did fulfilled the requirements of Hebrew law and, in addition, appeared to serve the higher purposes of God.[1]
>
> —W. Gunther Plaut

Scripture References

Genesis 38; Ruth 4; 1 Chronicles 2; Matthew 1

Biography

The story of Joseph is left dangling in midair when Moses unexpectedly veers off into the life of Judah in Genesis 38. This change of direction seems very random, but does fit better when viewed in the context of Jacob's life and legacy. It is here that Tamar emerges as an interesting character who is ultimately named in the lineage of Jesus Christ in Matthew 1.

Judah was one of the twelve sons of Jacob, and took for himself a Canaanite woman who bore him three sons. Tamar was chosen by Judah to be the wife of his firstborn son, Er, but the Bible says God took Er's life because of his wickedness.

To fulfill the custom of that time, Judah gave Tamar to his next son, Onan, so that they could have offspring and carry on the lineage of Er. Onan went through the motions of taking Tamar as his wife, but he was also wicked because he did not want to have children that would legally be seen as his brother's children. Onan deliberately spilled his semen on the ground so that Tamar would not be able to conceive, and this wickedness led to God taking his life as well.

After the deaths of his first two sons, Judah was afraid that his last son, Shelah, would be killed as well. He promised Tamar that when Shelah was old enough he would allow them to marry so that Tamar could at last conceive a child, and then sent her back to her father's house to wait.

After a long time passed and Shelah had grown up, Judah still had not kept his promise to let Tamar marry his last son. Tamar was still living at her father's house and learned that Judah was going to travel to Timnah to his sheepshearers, so she quickly devised a plan by which she could get for herself what had long been promised. She put on a veil and pretended to be a prostitute along the road to Timnah. When Judah saw her, he propositioned her, not knowing that the prostitute was actually his daughter-in-law, and promised to send a young goat as payment. Until such time as the payment could be delivered, Tamar took from Judah a pledge—his signet, cord, and staff.

Judah and Tamar had sex, and he returned home. When Judah sent the young goat as payment, Tamar was nowhere to be found. She had left the side of the road, traded her veil for her widow's garments, and gone back to her father's household. The result of this encounter was that Tamar had finally conceived a child.

Three months later, Judah heard the news that Tamar had presumably been promiscuous and gotten pregnant. As was the custom at that time, Judah demanded that his sinful daughter-in-law be brought out and burned for her transgression. As Tamar was being led to her execution, she revealed that she was pregnant by the man who had given her the signet, cord, and staff that were still in her possession. Judah was immediately convicted of his treachery when he saw his possessions and said, "She is more righteous than I, since I did not give her to my son Shelah" (Genesis 38:26).

Tamar had conceived twin boys by Judah and gave birth to Perez and Zerah. She is mentioned as the mother of Perez in Ruth 4, 1 Chronicles 2, and Matthew 1.

Role in Redemption

The story of Tamar forces the student of the Scriptures to do something that might be considered uncomfortable—resist the urge for a clean and tidy story. The story of Tamar is not a sitcom with a hilarious plot in which the heroine is never really in danger and the whole thing is tied up in a nice little bow before the end credits roll. No, Tamar lived a difficult life; there was rejection, danger, and darkness.

At least for other women, such as Sarah, there is a clear distinction between light and darkness. When Sarah had faith and obeyed, God proved to be faithful. When Sarah doubted and tried to solve matters on her own, it only brought pain and heartache. The world of Tamar had no such clearly defined parameters.

Her first husband, Er, was killed by God for his extreme wickedness. Those are all the details the passage provides. No matter how much our curiosity cries for more information, the specifics of how and why are never answered. One safe assumption might be that marriage to a man so wicked that God destroyed him would have been a horrific union at best.

What was supposed to happen next was for Tamar and her brother-in-law to produce a child who would be reared as Er's child. This levirate (*levirate* from the word for "brother-in-law") tradition would later become part of God's law for Israel (Deuteronomy 25:5–10), but at this time it seems to have been more of an unofficial cultural expectation. Nevertheless, more pain was inflicted on Tamar as her brother-in-law interrupted his relations with Tamar to ensure that she would not get pregnant. As Old Testament scholar Derek Kidner points out, Onan's treachery was worse than it might first appear. "Most English versions fail to make clear that this was his *persistent* practice. *When* should be translated *whenever*."[2] Not only did Onan refuse to fulfill his obligations to Tamar, he did it in the most excruciating way possible, and he did it repeatedly. Er was wicked, but Onan may have been even worse. God killed him as well.

Judah clearly lacked a lot in the areas of fatherhood and personal integrity, but even he could see a pattern developing. Judah refused to allow his third son to fulfill the necessary obligation, and thus Tamar, a widow in a world dependent on a man's presence in her life, was left alone and vulnerable.

Tamar's solution to the problem, pretending to be a prostitute in order to get pregnant by her father-in-law, was the plan of an understandably desperate woman. Interestingly, the book of Genesis gives no commentary on her decision-making. There is no condemnation or commendation; nothing but the facts. Did God approve of Tamar's methodology? It seems likely that He did not. Did God disapprove of her attempt to solve her problems? The text does not articulate God's thoughts. In some ways Tamar's story asks more questions than it answers.

Maybe our desire to know a little more about Tamar points us to something very important in Tamar's story. Her story is not really about how she survived the horrible things that happened to her. It isn't about what she did to get herself out of her situation. And it isn't even about the wickedness that she confronted. Ultimately, Tamar's story is a beacon of light pointing not in the direction of what a person can do, but what God can do with a person. Through her son Perez, Tamar would be an ancestor of Christ. Her dejection would give way to a permanent place as a woman of faith. She would be in the line of the Savior who came to destroy darkness and defeat sin.

By the Numbers

Number of children born to Tamar: 2

Number of sons of Judah killed by God: 2

Number of sons of Judah: 3

Things We Wondered

What did God think about Tamar's attempts to solve her problem?

What did Er do that was so evil?

Should Judah have taken a more active role in caring for Tamar while she waited for Shelah to come of age? Was it wrong that he sent her back to her parents' house?

4

Jochebed

The Disobedient Slave

When Moses relates how his mother made and prepared an ark, he hints that the father was so overwhelmed with sorrow as to be incapable of doing anything. Thus the power of the Lord more clearly manifested itself, when the mother, her husband being entirely disheartened, took the whole burden on herself. For, if they had acted in concert, Moses would not have assigned the whole praise to his mother. The Apostle, indeed, (Hebrews 11:23) gives a share of the praise to the husband, and not undeservedly, since it is probable that the child was not hidden without his cognizance and approval. But God, who generally "chooses the weak things of the world," strengthened with the power of his Spirit a woman rather than a man, to stand foremost in the matter.[1]

—John Calvin

Scripture References

Exodus 1, 2, 6; Numbers 26; Hebrews 11

Biography

Jochebed is best known for her God-given role as the mother of Moses. She and her husband, Amram—who also happened to be her nephew—were both from the tribe of Levi. To best understand Jochebed's story, one has to rewind history a bit and view some of the history of Israel as it relates to the nation settling in Egypt.

In a long and winding story, which can only be described as God's intricate plan for His people, Joseph (a son of Jacob) becomes a great leader in the land of Egypt and saves the Israelites from famine by providing them a way to leave starving Canaan and settle in Egypt. Upon their arrival, they were warmly welcomed by Pharaoh because of his great esteem for Joseph; however, after many years, a new king arose who did not know Joseph and felt no particular love for the nation of Israel. In fact, he felt threatened by the sheer number of Israelites and feared that they would align with Egypt's enemies in time of war.

This fear led Pharaoh to oppress the Israelites so he could keep control of them. He forced them to work as slaves in hard labor, building cities, tending the fields, and afflicting them with heavy burdens. Although His chosen people were in slavery, God had not forgotten about them, and was indeed still protecting them and providing for them. Exodus 1:12 says, "But the more they were oppressed, the more they multiplied and the more they spread abroad. And the Egyptians were in dread of the people of Israel."

In an effort to keep the Hebrews from multiplying, Pharaoh attempted to have Hebrew midwives kill any male babies as they were born. When the midwives obeyed God rather than Pharaoh and refused to kill the babies, Pharaoh commanded the Egyptian people to throw male Hebrew babies into the Nile River, but the female babies he allowed to be kept alive.

It is unclear if Jochebed was born into slavery in Egypt or if the oppression came about during her lifetime, but it seems more likely to be the latter. The reason for this conclusion is that Aaron was the older brother of Moses (Exodus 7:7), and Jochebed did not need to hide Aaron in secrecy to save his life the way she did for Moses. Thus, Pharaoh's paranoia and increasingly hostile treatment of the Hebrews arose after Aaron's birth but before Moses' birth. Jochebed also gave birth to a daughter, whom she named Miriam.

The Bible says that Jochebed gave birth to a baby boy and hid him for three months. When the child could no longer be hidden, she made a floating basket and placed it and the baby in the Nile River. Jochebed sent Miriam to follow the basket and see where it would end up. Again, God intervened and protected the baby by ordaining that Pharaoh's daughter find the basket and rescue him from the river. Thinking quickly, Miriam asked Pharaoh's daughter if she needed someone to nurse the child. Pharoah's daughter agreed, and so Jochebed nursed her son until he was ready to be weaned. At that time, Jochebed returned the baby to Pharaoh's daughter, who named the boy Moses.

Other than being mentioned in the genealogies of Moses and Aaron in Exodus 6, and listed as part of a census of Israel in Numbers 26, the last reference to Jochebed in Scripture is found in Hebrews 11:23, which affirms her great faith in God.

Role in Redemption

The role that Jochebed played in God's plan of redemption is one of the more unique stories that you will find. She was the mother of Moses, perhaps the greatest man ever to live outside of Jesus himself. In the Old Testament, David and Elijah were both significant figures to be sure, but the case can certainly be made that the figure of Moses looms large over every other person in Israel's history.

With such a noteworthy son, one could be forgiven for expecting Jochebed's contribution to redemption to be the story of an all-star mother who lived a life that was a textbook for mothers everywhere. Most of us anticipate that in order to raise a Moses, Jochebed must have been the greatest mom in history. That expectation, however, is not realized by the picture the Scriptures paint of Jochebed.

It isn't that the Bible describes Jochebed as a bad mother—far from it. Compared to the lives of many of the other compelling women in the Bible, there is little negativity in what is known of her. She does not bear the mark of scandal like Sarah and Tamar. She is not primarily remembered for one bad deed like Eve. The truth is that it is hard to get much of a pattern from Jochebed at all. She gave birth to Moses but only raised him until he was weaned. No doubt those years were impactful, but were they enough to have a real influence?

For all that we don't know about Jochebed, there are two often-overlooked aspects of her life that God used greatly.

First, she shows a tremendous capability to play the hand that she is dealt. Clearly, we do not know much about the private thoughts and feelings of Jochebed, whether her actions were begrudging, or if she was emotionally broken. What we do know is that rather than fixating on the motherhood and life that she no doubt would have wanted, she made the best of what she had. She hid her baby boy for as long as possible. When the time came that he could no longer be hidden, she turned her son over to God's sovereignty and set him adrift in the Nile. These are not the actions that any mother would wish for, but they are the actions of a mother who has come to accept the unthinkable—both the reality of her situation and God's hand in her affairs, even when those affairs are very troubling.

Second, Jochebed shows a characteristic that time and again women being used by God exhibit—bravery in the face of significant danger. The actions of Jochebed show that she very quickly acknowledged the facts of the situation she faced, and when it came down to it, she did not flinch in the face of daunting adversity. Pharaoh and the Egyptians made her and all her people slaves. They wanted her infant son to be thrown into the Nile River and be allowed to drown. Going against the commands of Pharaoh was to write one's own death warrant. Yet Jochebed risked everything for the life of her son. The writer of Hebrews sums it up this way: "By faith Moses' parents hid him for three months after he was born, because they saw he was no ordinary child, and they were not afraid of the king's edict" (Hebrews 11:23 NIV). With a tidal wave of danger bearing down upon her, Jochebed reacted like a woman whose faith in God obscured her fear of Pharaoh. Apparently this type of faith can impact a child, and the whole world, in just a few short years.

By the Numbers

Number of children born to Jochebed: 3

Months old Moses was when Jochebed set him afloat in the Nile in a basket: 3

Hebrew midwives listed in Exodus 1 who disobeyed Pharaoh: 2

Things We Wondered

How was it possible for Jochebed to hide Moses for three months? Did he never cry? How did she hide the extra dirty laundry?

How much did Jochebed get paid to nurse her own child? How old was Moses when Jochebed weaned him?

5

Zipporah

The Wife Who Saved Her Family

She did what Moses had failed to do. She found the courage to carry out what Moses could not. When Moses was lacking as the spiritual leader in his home, Zipporah rose up in faith and stood in the gap. Moses had failed to bring his firstborn son into the covenant with God. So Zipporah took the matter into her own hands because she feared God. Zipporah knew that God's judgment was on her husband. So she did what many women have done over the ages. She interposed herself between God's judgment and the person who was to be judged.[1]

—Tony Evans

Scripture References

Exodus 2, 4, 18

Biography

Zipporah, whose name means "bird," was one of seven daughters of Jethro (also called Reuel). Jethro was a shepherd and a priest of Midian, and was also a Cushite. His role as a priest of Midian indicates that he was a spiritual leader of his branch of the Midianites. Scripture does not make it clear, but it is possible that Jethro could have been a follower of the one true God. Certainly later on in Exodus he joined Moses and the Israelites in worshiping God with burnt offerings and sacrifices (Exodus 18:9–12). Thus, it is quite possible that Zipporah was raised to worship God and taught to fear Him.

Zipporah meets her soon-to-be husband when he goes on the run and ends up sitting down by a well in Midian. Moses had to flee Egypt and the wrath of Pharaoh when he killed an Egyptian man in defense of a Hebrew man. When he sat down by the well in Midian, Jethro's daughters came to water their father's flock at the well, but Moses again played the knight in shining armor, and came to the women's rescue when shepherds tried to drive them away from the well. Indeed, their chore was completed quickly when Moses lent his strong back to the task. A surprised Jethro asked his daughters how they were home so quickly from watering the flocks.

After hearing of Moses' kindness, Jethro sent his daughters to call Moses and extend the family's hospitality to him. Exodus does not tell us how much time passed, but Jethro eventually gave Zipporah to Moses as a wife, and she bore him two sons—Gershom and Eliezer—while they sojourned in Midian.

Moses continued to help Jethro tend his flocks, until one day God appeared to him in a burning bush at Horeb, the mountain of God. At this time, God instructed Moses to return to Egypt, for He wanted to deliver His people from their sufferings at the hands of the Egyptians. God assured Moses that the men who were seeking to kill him were themselves dead, and that the path to return to Egypt was clear. So Moses took his wife and their sons and went back to the land of Egypt.

While they were traveling, Zipporah and her family stopped at an inn, and the Bible says, "The Lord met him and sought to put him to death" (Exodus 4:24–25 NASB). To stay His divine hand, Zipporah quickly took a flint knife and circumcised her son on the spot and threw the foreskin at Moses' feet. She spoke to Moses, saying that he was "a bridegroom of blood," and the Lord relented and left Moses alone. This is a highly controversial and confusing incident, but it seems to be the climax in the life of Zipporah.

At some point Moses sent his wife and sons back to her father's house, but the reason for this is unknown. In Exodus 18, Jethro brings back Zipporah and their sons, and they are reunited with Moses in the wilderness, well after the Exodus. This is the last mention of Zipporah in Scripture.

Role in Redemption

Winston Churchill was speaking of Russia when he said, "It is a riddle wrapped in a mystery inside an enigma,"[2] but the phrase might more accurately describe Zipporah. Historians, scholars, and theologians have long struggled with just what to make of this woman whose appearances in the Scriptures are as brief as they are enigmatic. Zipporah appears in only three passages in all the Bible. It is as if her life is a play that takes place over the course of three acts, each of them progressively more puzzling than the last.

Perhaps the riddle of Zipporah has something to do with twenty-first-century stereotypes and tendencies to lump people into categories where they may or may not belong. When the curtain first pulls back on Zipporah, she is introduced as one of the seven daughters of the priest of Midian. Moses, fleeing from Egypt, plays the part of the knight in shining armor who protects and assists Zipporah and her sisters when they are harassed by shepherds as they attempted to draw water from the local well. All that is missing is some romantic tension, and this could be the beginning of the next romantic comedy at your local cinema. Typecasting Zipporah as a damsel in distress would be convenient, but as the curtain closes and the next scene begins we learn that it would be a complete misrepresentation of Zipporah and her story.

As simplistic as Zipporah's first act is, the second is baffling to the point of exasperation. As Zipporah, her husband, and her two sons are making their way from Midian to Egypt, God interrupts their journey. As the book of Exodus describes it, "The Lord met him and sought to put him to death." God's issue is that at least one of Moses and Zipporah's sons was uncircumcised. Moses, as the leader of his family, has very quickly gone from hero to bumbling sitcom dad, and it is only Zipporah's quick actions that prevent disaster. The passage is not clear, but the strongest possibility is that God was seeking to put Moses to death, but there is a school of thought that suggests that God was actually looking to kill the son. Either way, it is Zipporah's rapid reaction that saved the life of someone she loved. We can only surmise Zipporah's family was grateful, and that her son's relationship with his mom was a bit awkward for a while.

This is one of the stranger incidents of the Old Testament, but the heart of this story is not difficult to comprehend. Moses, tasked by God with leading the nation of Israel out of the land of Egypt, had failed to follow God's commands for the children of Abraham in Genesis 17. By failing to circumcise at least one of his sons, Moses forced God to take action. Moses' inaction had placed his family in mortal danger. Where there should have been obedience, there was only a void. Into this void stepped Zipporah.

Various commentators have proposed theories as to why one of Moses and Zipporah's sons was not circumcised. Some have suggested that the emphasis on firstborn sons in Exodus 4 indicates that Gershom was the son who was in need of circumcision. Other scholars suggest that Eliezer was the son in question. Old Testament scholar Ron Allen proposes this as a plausible background for Zipporah's emergency circumcision of one of her sons:

> When Gershom was born, Moses would have circumcised him on his eighth day as a matter of course, following the clear teaching of Genesis 17:9–14. While circumcision was also practiced by the Midianites, it would have been a kind of puberty "rite of passage" for them (and other Semitic peoples as well). Thus to the child's mother, the practice of circumcising babies would have been unexpected at best and abhorrent at worst. When the second child was born, Zipporah (perhaps in association with her father) may have strongly resisted, saying, "You have done this with the first boy, but not again. Not with my son." If only one son had not been circumcised, it would seem more likely to be the younger rather than the older.[3]

Though far from certain, this scenario at least gives a plausible explanation as to why Moses had neglected his duty in circumcising a son.

Whatever the reasoning behind Moses' failure, he found himself facing mortality on the road to Egypt. Had it not been for his wife, the story of Moses, the legendary stature that he alone occupies in the Old Testament, would have never existed. Without Zipporah's actions, history would have looked quite different. The Exodus, the Ten Commandments, the first five books of the Old Testament, the entire basis of Judaism would have been identified with someone other than Moses.

Zipporah stepped into the void left by her husband and saved his life. Then the curtain closes and we know nothing of the emotions experienced by Moses and Zipporah. We have no record of whether this startling incident brought the couple closer or drove them apart. Zipporah's third and final act in the biblical record may give us a clue. For whatever reason, at some point after the incident at the inn, Moses sent his family away. It is not until the children of Israel are on their way to the promised land that they are reunited. Was Moses afraid for his family? Did Zipporah find God's expectations more than she could bear? There is really no way of knowing. Perhaps the cost of obedience was more than this marriage could bear, or perhaps not. What we do know is that Moses, his sons, and the entire nation of Israel owe their existence to one woman's bravery.

By the Numbers

Sons by Moses and Zipporah: 2

Sisters of Zipporah: 6

Things We Wondered

Was it unusual for a man like Moses to help young women drawing water at the well?

Why did Moses send Zipporah and their sons home to live with Jethro?

Which son did Zipporah circumcise when God threatened to kill them?

How did Zipporah's emergency circumcision affect her marriage with Moses?

6

Rahab

The Abettor

Rahab the harlot. How dare the writer of Hebrews include this woman of ill repute in so noble a list of God's saints? Abel, Noah, Abraham, Sarah, Moses—yes. But Rahab! One can understand including "Rahab the Sunday school teacher," or "Rahab the missionary" . . . among the saints, but Rahab the harlot! What's more, her name crops up in an even more surprising context. In Matthew's genealogy of Jesus' forebears, there she is again (Matt. 1:5). Rahab, wife of Salmon, mother of Boaz, great-great-great-grandmama of our Lord himself. It's enough to make a person think. If Rahab the harlot can be a saint, anybody can.[1]

—William H. Willimon

Scripture References

Joshua 2–3; 6; Matthew 1; Hebrews 11; James 2

Biography

After the Israelites had wandered in the wilderness for forty years, and Moses had died in the land of Moab, God commissioned Joshua as the leader of the Israelites. He was "full of the spirit of wisdom" and guided the people to obey all that the Lord commanded (Deuteronomy 34:9). The Israelites finally possessed the promised land as a result of Joshua's leadership, and God's promises to Abraham were ultimately fulfilled.

Rahab, a prostitute in the city of Jericho, entered the story when she encountered two spies sent by Joshua to view the land, and especially the city of Jericho. These two men were on a mission to spy out the land and gather information for Joshua to aid him in planning an invasion of the land. While in Jericho, the spies found a place to lodge in the home of Rahab, which was built into the wall of the city. A later Jewish historian by the name of Josephus claimed that Rahab ran an inn, but it may have been the custom of the time that brothels and inns both functioned out of the same location.

The presence of the spies was reported to the king of Jericho, who sent word to Rahab that she was to turn the men over to him. However, Rahab defied the king and chose to help the spies instead. She told the soldiers that the men had left the city gate when it was about to be dark and even went so far as to hasten the soldiers away, saying that they could probably overtake the spies if they hurried. So the soldiers left immediately and pursued the spies as far as the fords, which were about five miles from the city.

When the king's men had gone, Rahab took the two men up on her roof to hide them in the stalks of flax she had laid out. Before they lay down, she explained her actions, saying, "I know that the Lord has given you the land, and that the fear of you has fallen upon us, and that all the inhabitants of the land melt away before you" (Joshua 2:9). She continued, recounting how the people in Jericho had heard of the work of the Lord at the Red Sea, and how the two kings of the Amorites were destroyed. Rahab also described how the city of Jericho and the land as a whole were in great fear of the Israelites because of all the victories God had given them on their journey to the promised land. She acknowledged the deity and power of God in heaven and on earth. Indeed, Rahab's knowledge of the works of God spurred her on to faith in God, which gave her the foundation to turn her convictions into action when she helped the spies.

In exchange for helping the spies, Rahab asked that they deal kindly with her when they returned with the Israelites to overtake Jericho. Because Rahab had spared their lives, the spies promised to grant her request and spare the lives of her and her family in return.

After receiving the men's guarantee, Rahab lowered them down the wall by using a rope tied through a window. She also gave instructions on how to avoid the king's men so that they wouldn't be caught on their way back to the Israelites.

The men left, and Rahab tied a scarlet cord in the window of her home, in accordance with her agreement with the men. The cord would be a sign that all in that house were to be spared. In so doing, Rahab and her family were saved from destruction.

This is the last we hear of Rahab, except when she is mentioned in the genealogy of Jesus in Matthew 1:5. Though it is not one hundred percent certain that they are the same woman, it is most likely that this same Rahab is the one mentioned in the passage on the lineage of Jesus.

Role in Redemption

Rahab had less going for her than just about any woman in the Old Testament. She was a prostitute, and she was a Canaanite.

Those two factors placed Rahab squarely in the sights of the Israelite army as it began to conquer the promised land. Her location in Jericho, living along the wall, made the danger of her situation all too real when the Israelite army suddenly showed up on the horizon. Her morality placed her on the wrong side of God's law, and her lineage placed her in the midst of a people that did not worship the one true God. Yet there was much more to Rahab than one might imagine.

Somewhere along the line the pagan prostitute had become a believer in God. Turning to God meant that she turned from her people, and in a move that would have been considered traitorous by her fellow citizens, she hid the spies sent to spy out her walled city for destruction. Rahab's method of keeping the spies hidden was to use a nifty piece of espionage—she lied and said they went the other way.

Rahab's method of protecting the spies, by being dishonest, has caused no small amount of consternation over the centuries. Was her lie still a sin if it was told to protect Hebrew spies? Can a lie, something the Scriptures repeatedly label as sin, ever be ethical? Throughout church history some have found Rahab's actions permissible because of the motivation behind them, saving the life of the Jewish spies and facilitating their conquering of the promised land. Yet theological luminaries such as John Calvin and Augustine had no small amount of difficulty with Rahab's dishonesty.

Calvin, for example, took Rahab to task for her actions, saying,

> As to the falsehood, we must admit that though it was done for a good purpose, it was not free from fault. For those who hold what is called a dutiful lie to be altogether excusable, do not sufficiently consider how precious truth is in the sight of God. Therefore, although our purpose be to assist our brethren, to consult for their safety and relieve them, it never can be lawful

> to lie, because that cannot be right which is contrary to the nature of God. And God is truth.[2]

Whatever one concludes about her methodology, there can be no doubt that Rahab was a woman of faith. She believed in the God of Israel so strongly that she was willing to risk everything to save herself and her family. Considering that Rahab had little in the way of information, or more to the point, revelation about God, the depth of her faith is staggering. Where many have evidenced little faith in spite of many words from God, Rahab exhibited a robust faith with little more than what we would consider rumors or hearsay to guide her.

The New Testament shows that the role that Rahab played was twofold: First, Rahab is listed in Hebrews 11, a chapter that lists many of the great accomplishments of faith by people of God. This is surprising on a number of levels, but it is very clear that Rahab (and by extension her family) did not die with the rest of Jericho because of her faith. In the previous verse it says, "By faith the walls of Jericho fell down after they had been encircled for seven days" (Hebrews 11:30). There is something interesting here that should not be missed. Rahab's faith was important not because *God* needed it, but because *she* did. Ultimately, the report of the spies was of little military value. God brought down the walls of Jericho not through some brilliantly conceived attack, but rather through miraculous means. Rahab's faith in protecting the spies was not the method that God used to benefit the Israelites, but rather it was what He used to benefit Rahab. When Rahab was helping the spies, she was also helping herself.

Second, in James 2:24–25, we see Rahab commended for a distinctly different part of what she did. The verses say,

> You see that a person is considered righteous by what they do and not by faith alone. In the same way, was not even Rahab the

> prostitute considered righteous for what she did when she gave lodging to the spies and sent them off in a different direction?
>
> NIV

The exact same action evidenced both faith and good works in the life of Rahab. Her faith motivated her to do the right thing. In this respect she earned great honor. The book of James gives one other example of good works: Abraham. On one side of the ledger is Abraham, father of the nation of Israel, revered almost without peer in the nation of Israel. On the other side of the ledger, we see the Canaanite prostitute. And Rahab is considered his equal in both faith and works.

She tried to save the Israelites and ended up saving herself in the process.

By the Numbers

Number of spies saved by Rahab: 2

Scarlet cord hung in the window by Rahab as a sign: 1

Days the Jewish spies hid in the hills until it was safe to continue to the Israelite camp: 3

Things We Wondered

Was it wrong for Rahab to lie about the spies being in her home?

How did Rahab hear of God in the first place?

How did Rahab feel about the fact that her faith would require that she betray the people of her city?

7

Deborah

The Exceptional Judge

God raised up a courageous woman named Deborah ("bee") to be the judge in the land. This was an act of grace, but it was also an act of humiliation for the Jews, for they lived in a male-dominated society that wanted only mature male leadership. "As for My people, children are their oppressors, and women rule over them" (Isaiah 3:12 NKJV). For God to give His people a woman judge was to treat them like little children, which is exactly what they were when it came to spiritual things.[1]

—Warren Wiersbe

Scripture References

Judges 4, 5; Hebrews 11

Biography

Deborah is a strong and faithful woman who wears a number of different hats in her short appearance in the book of Judges. The Bible presents her as a prophetess, a wife, a judge, a military leader, a historian, and a poet. She gives quite an impression while leading the Israelites to follow God.

The period of the Judges occurred after the nation of Israel was led by Joshua and before it was ruled by kings. It is during this time that the Israelites seem to be caught in a cycle of their choosing, as they repeatedly move through four states: (1) they turn from worshiping the one true God and instead worship idols; (2) as a result of their idolatry and sin, God turns them over to oppression by surrounding nations; (3) Israel repents of their sins and cries to God for help; (4) God delivers Israel by raising up a judge who leads them to freedom from their oppression. It is notable that the book of Judges describes seven such cycles of sin and redemption, and names twelve different judges who led the people of Israel.

After a judge named Ehud died, the Israelites once again succumbed to evil and the cycle recommenced. This time, God turned the nation of Israel over to Jabin, the king of Canaan, who reigned in Hazor. The commander of Jabin's armies was a man named Sisera, who delighted in the cruel oppression of the Israelites for twenty years. Sisera dominated the flatlands of Canaan with 900 chariots of iron, so the people of Israel began to primarily populate the hill country in that region.

During this ruthless regime, a woman named Deborah, who was the wife of Lappidoth, was judging Israel. She was one of a handful of women in the entire Old Testament referred to as a prophetess. A prophet or prophetess was a spokesperson for God, communicating a specific message from God to a designated audience. In her role as prophetess, Deborah reiterated

God's commands to a military commander named Barak and told him that he was to gather 10,000 men at Mount Tabor so that Sisera could be overthrown.

Barak agreed to follow God's command, but only if Deborah accompanied him. Whether Barak's hesitation to unquestioningly obey God was founded in fear or something else, it was clear that Deborah's presence would bring great courage and comfort to the men of Israel as they battled the Canaanites. The Israelites routed Sisera and his chariots in a stirring victory handed them by God.

The fifth chapter of Judges is a poem written as a celebration of the victory God gave Deborah and Barak. It is known as the song of Deborah and describes the provision and victory of the Lord, both in the history of Israel and in the battle against Sisera. After this epic battle, the land and its people rested for forty years.

Role in Redemption

The story of Deborah displays some rare insights into the character and heart of God. It is true that the lives of each and every woman in this book speak to who God is and how He works, but the life of Deborah, perhaps more than any other woman in the Bible, gives one a rare peek into the many varied methods that God uses.

First, we see that God can, and often will, choose to work in what seems to be the most unusual way possible. He is not restrained by rules or regulations. God's holiness demands that He will never sin, but everything else is subject only to His magnificent imagination. In other words, the only thing that can limit God is God himself.

The fact that thousands of years later Deborah's story is well-known is somewhat surprising. One lone woman from the tribe of Ephraim should never have had the power and influence of a judge. Or at least that is the preconceived notion with which many of us approach the text. She was a woman who lived in a world dominated by men. Even some God-ordained roles were limited by Him to being performed by men. The priesthood, for example, was closed to women and to men from any tribe other than Levi (Exodus 28:1). The position of judge, however, had no such restrictions. Deuteronomy 1 gives some instructions for judges that Moses put into place in each tribe, but the judges in the biblical book by that name were not fulfilling that role. The role of judge, of which Deborah was one, that we see before the kingdom of Israel was united by a king, seems to be something of an ad hoc position with little or no qualifications other than whom God decided to use. Yet Deborah is the only female judge in the entire Old Testament. Clearly, given Deborah's performance, a woman was more than capable of performing the job admirably, but God only chose one woman for the task. Why only Deborah? Why were no other women chosen as judges? As is often the case, the Creator does not feel the need to explain himself to His creation. Deborah was unique in the most literal way possible. The story of Deborah does not fit well in a box; it does not hold up well when it is stretched to further agendas. As much as anything, it is almost as if God gathered His angelic hosts and proclaimed, "Watch what I am going to do here. No one will see this coming!"

Second, Deborah is one of the most amazing examples of how God can and will work through the most mundane, obvious, and pedestrian methods. It is easy to be unfair to characters in the Scriptures when few of us would have done better under the circumstances, but the military commander Barak who was a contemporary of Deborah does not fare well in this story. God commanded him to battle Sisera, but there was no movement on Barak's part until Deborah promised that she would accompany him. The price that Barak would pay for his lack of courage was that he would not receive the acclaim for the victory; that recognition would go to a woman. You assume it will be Deborah but learn later that another woman, who actually accomplished the deed of killing Sisera, would receive the glory.

What is rather curious about the battle that ensued was the plan that God, via Deborah, communicated to Barak. Facing 900 chariots, the battle plan was something along the lines of "Take the high ground and fight from there." To which every student of military history says, "No kidding!" For thousands of years, fighting from the high ground has been the gold standard by which military campaigns are waged. In the book *The Art of War*, the ancient Chinese general and military strategist Sun Tzu had this to say: "All armies prefer high ground to low and sunny places to dark."[2] The idea that the divine revelation from God was to do something that every general for thousands of years would have suggested shows God's sense of humor, and how at times we can overcomplicate obedience. There are certainly times that faith means doing what is uncomfortable and maybe even scary, but there are also plenty of times that a life of faith means exercising wisdom and discernment and common sense. Deborah stands in stark contrast to Barak. The military man who should have seen the clear astuteness of God's command was trumped by Deborah, who believed all that was necessary was to do what God said.

It is in the life of Deborah that God shows us clearly that He is not constrained in how He works. Sometimes life's greatest victories will come about through miraculous and unexpected events, and sometimes they will be won through simple, uncomplicated consistency and faithfulness.

By the Numbers

Chariots of iron possessed by Sisera with which he oppressed the people of Israel: 900

Women referred to as prophetesses in the Old Testament: 5

Number of men Deborah directed Barak to assemble to fight Sisera: 10,000

Years of rest for the Israelites after the judgeship of Deborah: 40

Things We Wondered

How/why was Deborah named a judge over Israel in the first place?

Did Deborah have children?

What did Deborah's husband think of her position of leadership and authority among the Israelites?

8

Ruth

The Faithful Foreigner

I would particularly observe that wherein the virtuousness of her [Ruth's] resolution consists, viz, that it was for the sake of the God of Israel, and that she might be one of his people, that she was thus resolved to cleave to Naomi: "Thy people shall be my people, and thy God, my God." It was for God's sake that she did thus; and therefore her so doing is afterwards spoken of as a virtuous behavior in her . . . She left her father and mother, and the land of her nativity, to come and trust under the shadow of God's wings; and she had indeed a full reward given her, as Boaz wished; for besides immediate spiritual blessings to her own soul, and eternal rewards in another world, she was rewarded with plentiful, and prosperous outward circumstances, in the family of Boaz; and God raised up David and Solomon of her seed, and established the crown of Israel (the people that she chose before her own people) in her posterity, and (which is much more) of her seed he raised up Jesus Christ, in whom all the families of the earth are blessed.[1]

—Jonathan Edwards

Scripture References

Ruth 1–4; Matthew 1:5

Biography

Ruth is another of the women mentioned in the lineage of Jesus, and is known for her loyalty and kindness. She was a foreigner who married an Israelite, and showed a good deal of love, fidelity, and steadfastness when it mattered most.

There is some uncertainty about when the events found in the book of Ruth took place, but possibilities include during the lifetimes of Samson and the prophet Samuel, or during the days of Deborah, or possibly even the period of Gideon. The opening line of the book, which says, "In the days when the judges ruled there was a famine in the land" (Ruth 1:1), could indicate that it was during the time of the aforementioned individuals.

It was during the time of this famine that a man named Elimelech left his home in Bethlehem to find food and prosperity in the land of Moab. He took with him his wife, Naomi, and their two sons, Mahlon and Chilion. The mere fact that he left the land that was given to the Israelites by God and went to Moab, a land whose people worshiped idols and rejected the one true God, was an act of disobedience and disbelief.

While they were living in Moab, Elimelech died, leaving Naomi a widow. Mahlon and Chilion took for themselves wives from among the Moabite people, and the women's names were Orpah and Ruth. After another ten years, Naomi's sons died also, leaving her without her husband or her children.

After so much loss, Naomi decided to return to Israel. She urged her daughters-in-law to return to their mothers and remain in Moab so they could remarry. Orpah did as Naomi wished, kissed her good-bye, and went on her way; however,

Ruth clung to Naomi and remained steadfast in her pledge to stay with her mother-in-law. Despite further protests from Naomi, Ruth said,

> Do not urge me to leave you or to return from following you. For where you go I will go, and where you lodge I will lodge. Your people shall be my people, and your God my God. Where you die I will die, and there will I be buried. May the Lord do so to me and more also if anything but death parts me from you.
>
> Ruth 1:16–17

Naomi finally relented and allowed Ruth to travel back with her to Israel.

Although they returned to Israel, the two women were without husbands and had no one to provide for them. Ruth proposed a solution to this problem, to which Naomi gave her assent, and so Ruth went out to the barley fields that were being harvested in order to glean from them. This practice began when God commanded farmers in Israel not to harvest the corners of their fields, or strip their vineyards bare, so that the poor and needy could gather enough food to live (Leviticus 19:9–10; 23:22). Those who were "reapers" were free Israelites who agreed to glean from the fields for an agreed-upon price. As both a foreigner and a widow, Ruth was a suitable candidate for gleaning, although it must have been extremely strenuous and backbreaking work just to earn enough to live on.

Ruth arrived in the field of a man named Boaz, who happened to be a relative of Elimelech, Ruth's dead father-in-law. Unbeknownst to her, Boaz discreetly inquired into the identity of this unfamiliar woman and discovered the extreme sacrifice Ruth had made when she accompanied Naomi back to Israel. Being a compassionate and godly man, Boaz charged his servants to safeguard Ruth and provide for her by purposely leaving grain for her to glean. Boaz's concern for Ruth ensured that she would be well cared for and that she and Naomi would not starve. With a grateful heart, Ruth worked in Boaz's land, gleaning until the harvest was finished in the barley and wheat fields.

After the harvest was completed, Naomi urged Ruth to approach Boaz and seek his favor. Naomi was angling for Boaz to exercise his right as a kinsman-redeemer and thus marry Ruth and be a permanent provider for both of the women. Perhaps Naomi felt that Boaz was either shy or simply slow to act, but whatever the reason, she believed it necessary for Ruth to assert herself by expressing her desire to marry Boaz.

There is some theological debate as to whether Ruth's actions of seeking out Boaz on the threshing floor, uncovering his feet, and sleeping at his feet until morning were improper or simply a custom that was commonly practiced in Israel. What some may interpret as a conspiracy between Naomi and Ruth may simply be explained as an older Israelite woman educating a younger, foreign woman on Israel's social traditions.

Boaz may have been surprised by Ruth's hopeful approach, but he welcomed it nonetheless. His response to Ruth was: "May you be blessed by the Lord, my daughter. You have made this last kindness greater than the first in that you have not gone after young men, whether poor or rich" (Ruth 3:10). Acting with honor and integrity, Boaz acknowledged that a redeemer closer than he existed and should be given the right to marry Ruth first; but Boaz certainly gave Ruth assurances that marriage would be mutually agreeable and that he desired to redeem Ruth.

According to the Law, a kinsman-redeemer was a male relative who was to act on behalf of a relative who was in trouble, danger, or need of vindication. In Ruth's case, the kinsman-redeemer's pot was sweetened a bit by the plot of land that belonged to Elimelech, and which Naomi was going to sell. When asked if he was interested in purchasing this parcel of land, the closer relative said that he was indeed willing to be the redeemer for Naomi. And this was when Boaz revealed the details that he had kept hidden: "The day you buy the field from the hand of Naomi, you also acquire Ruth the Moabite, the widow of the dead, in order to perpetuate the name of the dead in his inheritance" (Ruth 4:5). Upon learning the whole of the arrangement, the closer relative declined to act on Ruth's behalf and the way was made clear for Boaz to marry Ruth.

The tension and drama that saturated Ruth's story seem to come to an abrupt halt with a happily-ever-after ending. Ruth and Boaz get married and are blessed with children, and this is when the great importance of Ruth's life is revealed. God gives Ruth and Boaz children, and so they become the great-grandparents of King David, and ultimately they are named in the lineage of Jesus.

Role in Redemption

The concept of an outsider is a common one. The twenty-first century has brought connectivity, but not necessarily connection. The modern world has enabled everyone to find their group or tribe, all from the comfort of their own home. Just because an information superhighway exists does not mean people actually travel it in groups.

People are still outsiders today, but there is something to be said for modernity at least softening the blow. In the time of Ruth, she found herself on the outside looking in economically, socially, and even religiously. As a widow whose only familial connection was her bitter mother-in-law, who was also a widow, she had little going for her. She had few resources to make money, and even as a believer in the one true God there were places in the temple that she was not allowed to go because she was not an Israelite by birth—once again an outsider.

There was no government agency to which Ruth could apply for aid. There was no Internet that allowed her to connect with people in similar circumstances. It wasn't as if she could just decide to go back to school on student loans to change her life's direction. No, the only thing Ruth could do was continue to endure the circumstances in which she found herself, on the outside looking in.

Had the world gotten its way, Ruth's story would have ended there. She would have been a down-on-her-luck widow who fell on hard times and who was victimized by a life and society that offered little opportunity for anyone, much less a young widow, to change her condition for the better. However, Ruth stands as a beacon of light in the Scriptures. Her story is a bright beam proclaiming that the world does not get its way.

In some ways Ruth's story resembles that of Tamar. Both women were candidates for redemption by someone called a kinsman-redeemer. Though the difference was that, in Ruth's case, this was no longer merely a social expectation, it was part of God's law for Israel. The fact that this concept was not something that Ruth initially pursued shows how much of an outsider she was. Tamar aggressively pursued protection through this obligation, but Ruth, and by extension Naomi, did not seem to consider it an option until divinely controlled circumstances brought it into focus.

Like any outsider, Ruth worked hard to make the most of every opportunity. Her situation on the outskirts of society was a dangerous one, and many then and now have found themselves taken advantage of or worse. Ruth is in a precarious position throughout the book that bears her name. It is not until the end of the book that the reader can finally breathe a sigh of relief on her behalf. What is just as clear in the four chapters that tell her story is that once Ruth put her faith in God, she was no longer an outsider. It was her faith that compelled her to cling to her mother-in-law. It was her faith that brought her to Israel. It was her faith that placed her on a path that she never saw coming.

Through the years, the concept of one plus God equals a majority has been attributed to many people, and no one seems to know for sure who said it or where it originated. The words may never have fallen from Ruth's lips, but her life gives testament to its veracity. Famine, poverty, destitution, fear, hunger, and death—all of these things were under God's control, and He ultimately accomplished His purposes in Ruth's life. She became the wife of Boaz, the great-grandmother of David, and the ancestor of Jesus. With family connections like those it would be hard to find someone ultimately more on the inside than Ruth.

Being all alone as an outsider is a terrifying experience, but with God an outsider does not stay that way for long.

By the Numbers

Ruth's husbands: 2

Sons listed in the Scriptures: 1

Approximate miles from Moab to Bethlehem: 30

Dry gallons of barley (approximate weight of an ephah) carried home by Ruth the first day she gleaned in Boaz's field: 5

Things We Wondered

As a prominent figure, and known as a compassionate and godly community leader, why wasn't Boaz already married?

How and when did Ruth come to believe in the one true God?

9

Naomi

The Bitter Mother-in-Law

> God does not evaluate human beings, and human history, and human events as we are prone to judge them and to evaluate them. A historian will note the crowning of a great king, but the Lord God will note the fall of a tiny sparrow [Matthew 10:29]. A historian will chronicle the marching of armies and the conquests of nations, but the Lord God will note the tears of a humble, poor peasant woman like Naomi.[1]
>
> —W. A. Criswell

Scripture References

Ruth 1–4

Biography

Intertwined with the life of Ruth is Naomi, her mother-in-law. She was the wife of Elimelech and the mother of Mahlon and

Chilion. Despite hardship and bitterness, Naomi was blessed by God and experienced the transformation of redemption in her life.

Naomi moved with her family from Bethlehem to Moab because of the famine, which is where her life was touched by loss and was changed forever. First, her husband passed away while they were living in Moab. Although this was tragic, Naomi was comforted, knowing that she had two sons who could provide for her and take care of her. But this safety net was taken away when both of her sons died also.

Naomi suddenly found herself with no way to provide for herself, much less the two daughters-in-law left in her charge after the deaths of her sons. She decided the best course of action was to allow Ruth and Orpah to return to their families in Moab, while she herself returned to Israel. Naomi knew that her own life now lacked security and comfort, and she wanted better for her daughters-in-law. She could not provide them with future husbands as she had no more sons, and she did not want them to descend into poverty with her.

Orpah acquiesced to Naomi's wishes and stayed in Moab, but Ruth pleaded to stay with Naomi. She passionately declared her allegiance to Naomi and pledged to follow her always, saying, "Where you go I will go, and where you lodge I will lodge. Your people shall be my people, and your God my God" (Ruth 1:16). In the face of such loyalty and devotion, Naomi relented and welcomed Ruth's company on the journey back to Israel. Their return caused quite a stir in the town of Bethlehem, and Naomi declared that they should call her *Mara*, which means "bitter." Indeed, she was quick to lay blame on the Lord for her bitterness, declaring that it was at God's behest that calamity was brought upon her. She said,

> Do not call me Naomi; call me Mara, for the Almighty has dealt very bitterly with me. I went away full, and the Lord has brought

> me back empty. Why call me Naomi, when the Lord has testified against me and the Almighty has brought calamity upon me?
>
> Ruth 1:20–21

Whether by chance or through strategic planning Naomi and Ruth arrived in Bethlehem at the beginning of the barley harvest. This gave them a means of survival, as Ruth could go to the fields and glean. On her first day of gleaning, Ruth made her way to a field owned by a man named Boaz. Ruth found favor with Boaz because of her faithfulness to Naomi, and so he made sure the two women were well looked after. Naomi encouraged Ruth to follow Boaz's instructions to stay close to his women, for her own protection and for the favor he could bestow on them. Naomi recognized Boaz as a close relative of her late husband and knew that he could redeem them according to Israel's custom.

In the next passage, Naomi shows care and concern for Ruth, just as Ruth first demonstrated to her. She lays out a meticulous plan for her daughter-in-law to approach Boaz on the threshing floor, which would signify to the gentleman that Ruth was willing to be redeemed and marry. This would guarantee security for Ruth and give her a second chance at a good marriage and children. Ruth was most likely not acquainted with the cultural norms in Israel that could lead to her redemption, but Naomi certainly was familiar.

Ruth followed Naomi's plan and soon discovered that Boaz was more than willing to act as her kinsman-redeemer. However, there was one small obstacle to overcome. There was another relative who was closer than Boaz, and who should be given the first option of acting as redeemer. The nearer relative declined the right of redeemer because it would put his own inheritance in jeopardy, and so the way was made clear for Boaz and Ruth to marry.

Naomi experienced a happy ending to the hardships, after all. She was blessed to have a grandchild through Ruth and Boaz, and her future was secure. The women of the city said to Naomi,

> Blessed be the Lord, who has not left you this day without a redeemer, and may his name be renowned in Israel! He shall be to you a restorer of life and a nourisher of your old age, for your daughter-in-law who loves you, who is more to you than seven sons, has given birth to him.
>
> Ruth 4:14–15

Role in Redemption

What might have been is the fertilizer of bitterness. The loss of a future that never came to be is one of the most difficult losses to endure. Surely as a young wife and mother, Naomi anticipated growing old in her homeland with Elimelech. No doubt she looked forward to the days when she would beam with pride watching the men her sons had become at family gatherings. Assuredly, at those same family gatherings, she would dutifully perform the role of matriarch surrounded by a host of beautiful, noisy, mischievous grandchildren. When she looked forward, Naomi saw love, laughter, and blessing.

It takes only a matter of seconds for a reader to enter the future that Naomi was not prepared for, but it took her years to slowly plummet from a promising future to an anguished present. The writer of Ruth gives us little insight into Elimelech's decision to leave Bethlehem. We don't know if Naomi agreed with his plan or not. Thousands of years later we know that it was the wrong choice, but in the moment, Elimilech made the choice he did. Today, the word *Bethlehem* gushes with meaning. *Bethlehem* means "David." *Bethlehem* means "Jesus." How could anyone leave a place so favored by God? But during the life of Naomi, Bethlehem was a sleepy little village with precious few resources to survive a famine of any substance. The modern reader, especially the one who knows the story, probably experiences something akin to watching a movie and seeing someone go into a room where danger awaits. Shouts of "No! Stop! Don't do it! Go back! What are you thinking?!" probably echo through your brain when you see the family of four ominously leave Judah.

Though not completely certain, one can surmise that Mahlon and Chilion were young when the family left Bethlehem, since both were unmarried. They moved to Moab, then their father died, and only after the loss of their father did the two boys come of age and marry. At some point after their marriages, each of the brothers followed their father into the grave. It would have taken some time for all of this to take place. Year after year Naomi's grief multiplied with every sorrowful disaster that shadowed her life.

It should not surprise us to find Naomi broken and bitter. After experiencing the loss of his beloved wife, C. S. Lewis was at times afraid that he would never recover, and his loss was not as compacted as that of Naomi. Reading of Lewis's agony . . .

> Part of every misery is, so to speak, the misery's shadow or reflection: the fact that you don't merely suffer but have to keep on thinking about the fact that you suffer. I not only live each endless day in grief, but live each day thinking about living each day in grief. . . . An odd byproduct of my loss is that I'm aware of being an embarrassment to everyone I meet. At work, at the club, in the street, I see people, as they approach me, trying to make up their minds whether they'll "say something about it" or not. I hate it if they do, and if they don't.[2]

. . . one gets but a glimpse of what must have been going through Naomi's mind.

Naomi's grief was crushing, her grief was ever-present, and her bitterness all too explainable and obvious. It is so obvious in fact that unlike most people she doesn't even bother trying to hide it. She tells people to call her Mara, a name that means bitter. Naomi isn't pretending to be okay with the hand she has been dealt. Her life is horrible, she blames God for it, and her anguish is such that she doesn't care who knows it.

In the midst of Naomi's gloom and darkness, however, a faint light began to glow. It wasn't even hope, at least not at first. In the beginning there was the daughter-in-law, in the throes of grief herself, who refused to leave. Then there was the unmistakable hand of providence, finding Boaz's field. Soon the bitterness was not gone, but at least she was not alone. Then there was the distant relative, wealthy and eager to help. In a short time a marriage takes place, and before you know it, Naomi is staring into the eyes of a beautiful baby grandson.

Make no mistake. Naomi's life did not magically fix itself. Her losses were inexplicable. The happiness and joy at the end does not negate the pain and anguish at the beginning. Naomi sustained heavy losses that left her scarred for life. Nothing replaces a lost spouse and lost children—nothing in the world. God did not instantly make it all better for Naomi. God did not take away the pain and sorrow, but He did chop down the tree of bitterness that had taken root in Naomi's heart.

At the beginning of the book of Ruth, Naomi tells the women of Bethlehem to call her Mara, meaning bitter. At the end of the book, the women of Bethlehem surround her and call her blessed. In between bitter and blessed is the heart of Naomi's story. The change in her attitude and outlook was not due to anything inside of her. She did not find courage through facing her demons. She did not read some self-help book for her self-esteem issues. No, what happened between bitter and blessed was the redemptive work of Almighty God. God reached down into the mess that was Naomi's life and orchestrated events to turn her tragedy into good fortune. Naomi's bleak future was the canvas upon which He would paint His masterpiece of redemption in her life for all to see.

By the Numbers

Husbands of Naomi who died: 1

Sons of Naomi who died: 2

Daughters-in-law of Naomi who remained in Moab: 1 of 2

Things We Wondered

How did Naomi feel about leaving Bethlehem and moving to Moab?

Did Naomi approve of her sons marrying Moabite women?

10

Hannah

The Infertile Woman

> Hannah asked, and the Lord heard. By this significant name, Samuel's life would always be linked to his mother's vow, and his prayers would always be colored by the knowledge that God hears.[1]
>
> —Tony W. Cartledge

Scripture References

1 Samuel 1 & 2

Biography

Hannah was one of two wives for a man named Elkanah, who lived at the end of the time of the Judges. Her husband's other wife was a woman named Peninnah, and they all lived in the hill country of Ephraim.

For a woman in ancient biblical times, being married and having children was an important aspect for security and position in society. Thus, the fact that Peninnah had children but Hannah had none caused Hannah a great deal of grief.

Elkanah feared God and followed the Law. He made a yearly pilgrimage to Shiloh, where he obediently worshiped and sacrificed to the Lord. In Shiloh, the priests of the Lord were Hophni and Phinehas, both sons of Eli. At the time of the sacrifice, Elkanah would give portions to Peninnah and their children together, but to Hannah he gave a double portion, because of his great love for her. The Bible says that Elkanah loved Hannah greatly, even though the Lord had closed her womb (1 Samuel 1:5).

The yearly sacrifices and offerings were a time of great turmoil for Hannah. Being childless, she was bullied and provoked by Peninnah. Hannah would become so distressed that she was moved to tears and refused to eat. Though Elkanah loved her and wanted her to be happy, he did not comprehend this agony and wished that Hannah would love him more than any sons she might have.

One year, after they had shared food and drink while on their pilgrimage to Shiloh, Hannah rose and went to the tabernacle. Weeping, she vowed to God,

> O Lord of hosts, if you will indeed look on the affliction of your servant and remember me and not forget your servant, but will give to your servant a son, then I will give him to the Lord all the days of his life, and no razor shall touch his head.
>
> 1 Samuel 1:11

Eli was the high priest and was there at the tabernacle, and witnessed her emotional prayer to God. He mistakenly thought her to be drunk because he saw her lips moving but heard no sound. Hannah assured the priest that she was not drunk, but was very troubled in spirit. She pleaded with him not to think ill of her, but to see her great sorrow and know that she was seeking the Lord. Eli saw the truth, and told Hannah to return home with the peace of knowing that God would grant her petition. And so Hannah returned home and ate and was no longer sad.

Hannah and her family rose early the next morning and returned to their house at Ramah after they had worshiped the Lord. After returning home, Hannah conceived and bore a son, whom she named Samuel.

Hannah raised Samuel until he was old enough to be weaned, which would have been around three years old. At that time, Hannah traveled with Samuel to the tabernacle at Shiloh, again for the yearly pilgrimage. She brought the child to Eli, along with a three-year-old bull, an ephah of flour, and a skin of wine. It is hard to imagine the strength and courage it took for Hannah to leave her son with Eli after longing for a child of her own for so long. But she fulfilled her vow to the Lord and returned Samuel to the Lord under the care of Eli.

Samuel stayed in the tabernacle and ministered before the Lord. Every year when Hannah accompanied Elkanah to worship at Shiloh, she would bring Samuel a new robe she had made for him. Eli would bless Elkanah and Hannah, saying, "May the Lord give you children by this woman for the petition she asked of the Lord" (1 Samuel 2:20). Hannah did conceive again and bore three sons and two daughters.

First Samuel 2:1–10 is known as Hannah's song of thanksgiving to the Lord.

Role in Redemption

"Are you listening?"

It is a phrase uttered by many an exasperated wife as she pours out her heart to her husband only to discover that while he may be physically present his mind is a million miles away. To be fair, the average husband is probably not the bumbling idiot portrayed on television who ignores his wife unless he wants sex and who will go to extreme lengths to avoid household chores. The best of marriages have had plenty of moments where a wife has asked, "Are you listening?" and a husband hurriedly tried to figure out what they had been talking about. Though the Bible clearly states that Elkanah loved Hannah, they do not appear to have had the best marriage.

In all fairness to Elkanah, he seems to be more oblivious than intentionally negligent. His wife struggles deeply with infertility and the barrage of insults hurled at her by Penninah. He does not understand that the statement "Am I not better to you than ten sons?" is at best woefully insensitive and at worst stunningly foolish.

Unfortunately for Hannah, the answer to her question seems to be no, Elkanah is not listening. She is the one in pain. She is the one praying for a son. She is the one going to the temple to pray. She is the one who is heartbroken. She appears to be the only one enduring the pain and suffering of her reality.

Elkanah may not have been listening, but he was not the only one to whom Hannah posed the question. When you read the story of Hannah, you cannot miss that she was even more desirous to know if God was listening. Hannah's pleading with God shows a woman in torment and distress. She was a woman attempting to carry the load of her trauma, and it was a load she simply could not carry alone.

Today, if we were present during Hannah's emotional prayer to God, we might suspect she was having a breakdown or some type of psychological episode. Certainly back in her day we would probably conclude, as did Eli, that there was some form of inebriation at play in the life of this woman. Either way we would all miss the point. Hannah was indeed having a breakdown; in fact, the breakdown had already occurred. Hannah had reached the point of being unable to carry the burdens that life had placed on her shoulders. She had gone as far as she could go on her own, and now, under extreme distress, she brought her issues to God. She wept and she pleaded, no doubt wondering if anyone was listening. Was God paying attention? Did He care? Would He respond on her behalf?

Hannah's life is a wonderful testament to the fact that God is most certainly listening to His children. He does not always answer in the way we would like. He does not always respond as quickly as we feel He should. Frequently, He does not even feel the need to explain himself. But He is always listening.

By the Numbers

Wives of Elkanah, of which Hannah was one: 2

Possible age when Samuel went to live in Shiloh with Eli and his sons: 3

Total number of children given to Hannah and Elkanah by God: 6

Things We Wondered

Why did the Lord close Hannah's womb in the first place?

Why does 1 Samuel 2:5 seem to indicate that Hannah had seven children, when the other verses indicate that she had six children?

How did Eli know that Hannah's prayer for a child would be granted by God?

How could Hannah leave Samuel with Eli when his two sons were known for being corrupt and evil?

11

Bathsheba

The Adulteress

> For when late in an evening he took a view round him from the roof of his royal palace, where he used to walk at that hour, he saw a woman washing herself in her own house: she was one of extraordinary beauty, and therein surpassed all other women; her name was Bathsheba.[1]
>
> —Titus Flavius Josephus

Scripture References

2 Samuel 11, 12; 1 Kings 1, 2; 1 Chronicles 3

Biography

Now we turn to look at the work of God's redemption in the life of Bathsheba, a woman torn between her husband and her king. Bathsheba was the daughter of Eliam, and the wife of

Uriah the Hittite. She was from the tribe of Judah and lived in Jerusalem during the time of King David's reign.

Uriah was one of King David's mighty men, which was a group of thirty-seven of David's best warriors. He fought under the leadership of Joab, who was the captain of David's entire army. During the spring one year, David stayed home while his army waged war against the Ammonites in the city of Rabbah. This is significant because in those days the role of the king was to lead the army in battle and not enjoy the luxury of home while his men were in the throes of war.

Late one afternoon, David was strolling along the roof of his palace, and from his vantage point happened to see Bathsheba as she was bathing. He was immediately drawn to her beauty and did not resist the temptation to learn more about her. David inquired after her identity and discovered that she was the wife of Uriah the Hittite. Rather than forgetting the woman altogether after learning she was married, he sent for her and slept with her.

This particular passage has sparked many heated debates regarding whether their physical intimacy was consensual. The Bible does not answer that question, but it is fair to say that David overstepped his bounds and used his position as king to get what he wanted. It is also obvious from 2 Samuel 12 that God laid the bulk of responsibility squarely on David's head for this sin.

After returning home, Bathsheba sent word to David that she was pregnant. David's reaction to this news was to "fix the problem" rather than confess his sin. This led to more sin compounding the original sin of adultery. David sent word to Joab that Uriah should be sent back to Jerusalem with a report of how the army was faring. The plan was to have Uriah return home, sleep with his wife, and thus conceal the affair. However, Uriah was an honorable and righteous man, and he refused to go to his house while his fellow soldiers were unable to do the same.

A few days passed, and David, seeing that his plan had failed, sent Uriah back to the battle with a message for Joab. The message instructed Joab to put Uriah on the front line of the battle and then order the army to draw back from him so that he would be struck down and killed. David's orders were followed, and Uriah the Hittite was killed in battle. Not only had David committed adultery and been deceitful, but now he added murder to his mounting sins.

Bathsheba observed a period of mourning for her fallen husband and then was taken to the palace and became the wife of King David, and she bore him a son. But this was not a happy ending to the story, for "the thing that David had done displeased the Lord" (2 Samuel 11:27).

God sent Nathan the prophet to rebuke David for his sins. Even though the king showed remorse and confessed that he had sinned against God, he and Bathsheba would both face the consequence of sin. Just as God had promised, the son of David and Bathsheba became sick and died. The Bible subtly emphasizes David's adultery by referring to Bathsheba as "Uriah's wife" in 2 Samuel 12:15, after she had already married David and given birth to his child.

Reflecting on Bathsheba's story up to this point, I [Elaina] can't help but feel pity and compassion for her. Both her husband and her son were taken away from her because of the sin of another man. And now she was married to this man and expected to build a life with him. It seems as if her life was not her own, and she was but a pawn in another man's hand.

David comforted Bathsheba and lay with her, and she again became pregnant and gave birth to another son. David called his name Solomon. Second Samuel 12:24–25 says, "And the Lord loved him and sent a message by Nathan the prophet. So he called his name Jedidiah, because of the Lord."

Although Bathsheba is not mentioned in the chapters that describe the rebellion of Absalom, it bears mentioning because it is part of the story of the throne of Israel. Absalom was a son of David by another wife, and he attempted to take the kingdom away from his father by playing on the affections of the Israelites. During this attempted coup, many people chose to follow Absalom, who had previously been loyal to David. This included Ahitophel, one of David's most trusted advisors and very likely Bathsheba's grandfather. Absalom's actions of betrayal fulfilled God's promise to judge David:

> "Now therefore the sword shall never depart from your house, because you have despised me and have taken the wife of Uriah the Hittite to be your wife." Thus says the Lord, "Behold, I will raise up evil against you out of your own house. And I will take your wives before your eyes and give them to your neighbor, and he shall lie with your wives in the sight of this sun. For you did it secretly, but I will do this thing before all Israel and before the sun."
>
> 2 Samuel 12:10–12

This rebellion was swiftly quashed and Absalom was killed, thus securing the throne for David.

Sometime later, when David was old and dying, it became clear that Adonijah was making a play to inherit the throne. Adonijah was another son of David by his wife Haggith, and the Bible says that David "had never at any time displeased him by asking, 'Why have you done thus and so?'" (1 Kings 1:6). It seems clear that exalting himself was par for the course with Adonijah, and his father, David, never had the time or inclination to check his self-indulgent attitude. Thus, when he made a move to wrest the kingdom from his own father, he was left unrestrained until Nathan the prophet stepped in.

Nathan informed Bathsheba about the situation so she could save her own life and the life of Solomon. If Adonijah were to take the throne, he would most likely seek to kill Bathsheba and Solomon because of their favored status with David, and out of fear that Solomon would rise up and usurp him someday. Nathan told her to approach David and remind him of his promise that Solomon, not any of David's other sons, would reign as king. David's response was to reaffirm his pledge to Bathsheba, and on that day Solomon was anointed as the next king of Israel.

After David died, Adonijah approached Bathsheba, asking for a favor. He asked if she would entreat Solomon on his behalf to have Abishag the Shunammite as his wife. Bathsheba did relay the request, but Solomon was wise and saw through the thinly veiled threat to his kingship. In those days, the women in the king's harem were considered property of the ruling king. If Adonijah had taken Abishag as his wife, when she had previously been a concubine of King David, it would have strengthened his claim to the throne, and perhaps given others reason to doubt Solomon's claim to the throne. Adonijah was again trying to take the throne away from the rightful king, except this time Solomon held him responsible for his sinful actions and executed him.

There has been some speculation among theologians as to whether Solomon was speaking of his mother when he wrote Proverbs 31. We can never be sure if Bathsheba is in fact the Proverbs 31 woman, but from her role in Scripture we can know for certain that she acted with honor and grace in the circumstances in which she found herself.

Role in Redemption

Sadly, as for many women in the Bible, history has not done well by Bathsheba. In the modern period she was the frequent subject of paintings. The reasons for this are articulated by Calvin Seminary professor Amanda W. Benckhuysen:

> Bathsheba was an immensely popular subject during the sixteenth and seventeenth centuries, providing artists with the irresistible challenge of capturing on canvas the extraordinary beauty of one who caused the great King David to fall. Furthermore, along with the daughters of Lot and Susanna, she provided artists of the time a legitimate excuse for trying their hand at representing the sensuous female nude. In this respect, she was an exquisite test of the artist's skill: the measure of the artist's success being the ability of the finished product to command the male gaze.

Among the numbers of artists fascinated by Bathsheba was the Dutch painter Rembrandt, who focused paintings on Bathsheba three times. The last of which, *Bathsheba at Her Bath*, is considered one of Rembrandt's best works.

In addition to having painter after painter depict her naked body, Bathsheba also makes an appearance in the novel *The Scarlet Letter* by Nathaniel Hawthorne. In the novel, the character of Reverend Dimmesdale commits adultery. In the story, Dimmesdale's house is decorated with a tapestry that Hawthorne describes as "representing the scriptural story of David and Bathsheba, and Nathan the prophet, in colors still unfaded, but which made the fair woman of the scene almost as grimly picturesque as the woe-denouncing seer."[2]

Bathsheba's reputation is based on reality, but one has to wonder if the extent to which she has been portrayed as the patron saint of adultery has not been both out of proportion to her mistakes and to the reality of what the Scriptures tell us about this woman. For thousands of years, Bathsheba was all too often portrayed as a seductress and the instrument of evil to bring down good King David. Today, in many instances, Bathsheba is viewed as a victim, a helpless pawn powerless to resist an evil and lusty king. It has been suggested by some that David and Bathsheba's sexual liaison was not consensual, but was rather the act of a powerful man forcing himself upon a woman.

With modern scholarship, the pendulum has thankfully swung, but it may have gone one step too far. It is most certainly true that Bathsheba was at a great disadvantage. David's power would have made it most difficult to say no if Bathsheba so desired. Still, it must be acknowledged that there was a Hebrew term for the physical act of rape, and it was not used in the story of David and Bathsheba. So did David physically force himself on Bathsheba? This does not seem to be what the Scriptures tell us, but we must be very clear that from what we see on the inspired pages of the Bible, God held David almost completely responsible. When the prophet Nathan confronts David about his sin, he repeatedly declares that David has "taken the wife of Uriah the Hittite to be your wife." It is very clear from Nathan's words that God did not hold Bathsheba responsible in the same way that He did David. Alexander Izuchukwu Abasili puts it well when he says,

> The great power difference between David and Bathsheba supports the interpretation that Bathsheba, rather than physically resisting the king, opted for a passive attitude. She saw herself in a situation in which her only option was to submit to the king's sexual passion. Within this context, Bathsheba's willingness is drastically reduced but not entirely extinguished. Consequently, Bathsheba, though a victim of circumstances may not be declared entirely innocent; she does share minimally in the responsibility.[3]

As is the case with many of the famous women of the Bible, Bathsheba's reputation has taken an unnecessary beating, which is far from in line with the spiritual reality. In Matthew's gospel, he mentions five women in the genealogy of Jesus, something rather unusual to begin with. Tamar and Rahab, like Bathsheba, are largely known for their own sketchy reputations. How interesting it is that God's sovereign plan for "the wife of Uriah," as Matthew refers to Bathsheba, was to use the one of David's eight wives with such a history to further the line of the Messiah. There were seven other options, but God saw fit to place Bathsheba in a place of honor and remembrance.

For thousands of years we've gotten the story of Bathsheba wrong. She was not the scarlet-letter bearer of the Old Testament. She is not the forever seductive nude figure in the paintings of Rembrandt and other painters. Bathsheba was the wife of Uriah, the mother of Solomon, and the ancestor of the Messiah.

By the Numbers

Number of husbands Bathsheba had: 2

Children who died at birth: 1

Known number of David's wives, including Bathsheba: 8

Children of David and Bathsheba who lived: 4

Things We Wondered

Did losing her husband and her son because of David's sinful choices cause Bathsheba to be bitter toward David?

Why didn't God just tell David and Bathsheba to name their son Jedidiah, as He told other people in the Bible?

Why did David's servants feel it was necessary to find Abishag to keep the king warm, instead of Bathsheba?

12

The Widow of Zarephath

The Obedient Gentile Widow

Her character will come out in due course, but there must have been something in her which could not be found in the many widows of the land of Israel (Luke 4:25–26). It was for no arbitrary reason that God passed them over, and went so far afield. She must have possessed qualities of character, germs of better things, sparks of heroism and faith, which distinguished her from all her sorrowing sisterhood and made her the befitting hostess of the prophet; the glad sharer with him in his Father's bounty.[1]

—F. B. Meyer

Scripture References

1 Kings 17; Luke 4

Biography

The story of the widow of Zarephath actually begins with the prophet Elijah. Elijah was a Tishbite and prophesied to King Ahab that there would be no rain or dew in Israel for three years. This proclamation of impending disaster for the nation was God's response to the wickedness of King Ahab. After he had spoken these words, God sent Elijah to hide by the brook Cherith, where he was fed by ravens twice each day and drank from the brook until it dried up. It was necessary for him to hide so that Ahab would not be able to find and kill him.

After the brook dried up, God spoke to Elijah, "Arise, go to Zarephath, which belongs to Sidon, and dwell there. Behold, I have commanded a widow there to feed you" (1 Kings 17:9). As Elijah approached the gate of the city, he saw a widow there gathering sticks. He called out to her to bring him water and some food, and her response was that she and her son had nothing to eat. Desperate and hungry, the widow had enough flour and oil left to make a small amount of bread. This was to be the last meal she and her son would eat before they died of starvation.

At first, Elijah's request to be fed and given water by a widow appears selfish and unfeeling. Widows were some of the poorest members of society, as they had no one to care for them, and so in times of want they often ran out of food first. Upon closer examination, however, you can see that Elijah was testing her mettle to see if this was indeed the widow described by God.

The widow's response to Elijah is truly astounding and full of faith. She acknowledges her belief in the living God and immediately complies with the prophet's request, without question or hesitation. This woman confidently placed her faith in God as Provider! The widow and her household ate for many days, and her flour and oil never ran out, just as God had promised.

Sometime later, the widow's son became very ill and died. In her grief, she lashed out at Elijah: "What have you against me, O man of God? You have come to me to bring my sin to remembrance and to cause the death of my son!" (1 Kings 17:18). Nothing is mentioned that lets us know specifically what she believes to be the sin in her life, but clearly the widow believes that God is punishing her by allowing her son to die.

Elijah performed his third miracle of this passage by taking up the son, crying out to God, and seeing God restore life to the boy. The widow's response is again a testimony of her faith in God: "Now I know that you are a man of God, and that the word of the Lord in your mouth is truth" (1 Kings 17:24).

The only other place in Scripture that mentions the widow of Zarephath is in Luke 4. Jesus is announcing himself to the nation of Israel as the Messiah and says that despite the presence of many widows in Israel, God sent Elijah to this particular Gentile woman. This is significant because it shows that God's plan of redemption was not limited to Israel, but includes all people.

Role in Redemption

Western culture in the twenty-first century is obsessed with rankings. A quick Internet search will reveal a "best of" list for almost everything imaginable. There is even a list of best "best of" lists. These lists are assembled and then people debate them. Consistently, one of the things about these lists is considering who was not ranked high enough, or to put it another way, who was underrated. On any list of women of the Bible, the widow from Zarephath is sure to be underrated.

The reason why this widow gets such scant attention is due largely to the fact that she appears so little in the Bible as to be almost invisible. One chapter in 1 Kings and two verses in Luke are the only times she is mentioned in the Scriptures. She may appear rarely, but when this woman is in a biblical story it is time to take notice.

Her place in the story of Elijah comes at a pivotal moment not just for the Old Testament's most renowned prophet, but for the nation of Israel. When she comes to the aid of Elijah, it is just before God sends him to challenge King Ahab, leading to a confrontation on Mount Carmel between Elijah and the prophets of the false god Baal. By the time that clash was over, 850 false prophets were dead and Elijah had called down fire from heaven.

Her role in the life of Elijah was significant, but his role in her life was just as important. Her son, who was raised from the dead by the prophet, is one of only a handful of resurrections to occur in the Bible, and he had the distinction of being the first.

The widow of Zarephath's singular appearance in the Old Testament is significant, but her brief mention by Jesus in Luke 4 is truly remarkable. The events of this passage occur at the very beginning of Jesus' ministry. He has chosen some disciples, been baptized by John the Baptist, turned water into wine, taught, and done some miracles. He is known in His home region of Galilee as well as the region of Judea, but the vast majority of the teaching and ministering that He would do was still in the future. In Luke 4, Jesus tells a synagogue full of people, many of whom had known Him for His entire life, that He was the promised Messiah. When they respond with a lack of faith, Jesus compares their lack of faith to that of Israel in the time of Elijah. When Jesus announces himself to His people and is summarily rejected by them as their Messiah, it is to the lowly, hardly mentioned widow of Zarephath that He turns. He responds to the unbelieving crowd, saying,

> Truly, I say to you, no prophet is acceptable in his hometown. But in truth, I tell you, there were many widows in Israel in the days of Elijah, when the heavens were shut up three years and six months, and a great famine came over all the land, and

> Elijah was sent to none of them but only to Zarephath, in the land of Sidon, to a woman who was a widow.
>
> Luke 4:25–26

Like so many of the women in the Bible, the widow of Zarephath was an outsider. She experienced great pain and loss, which were frequent companions of the women we have seen in this book. Yet Jesus used her as a primary exhibit of God's grace and intentions for humanity. Israel was God's chosen vehicle by which He would bring the Messiah to lost people, but God's plan was always much larger than one nation. When God's prophet needed food and water, He sent him to a Gentile widow. When God's Son was rejected, He appealed to the same Gentile widow. Rarely has God's grace blazed more brilliantly than in the life of one rarely mentioned widow.

By the Numbers

Years without rain promised by the prophet Elijah: 3

Sons by the widow of Zarephath: 1

Number of times Elijah stretched himself over the widow's dead son to bring him back to life: 3

Things We Wondered

Of all the people and creatures available to God, why did He choose ravens to be the means of feeding Elijah by the brook Cherith?

How old is the widow's son?

What is the sin the widow refers to when she grieves her son's death and claims responsibility?

13

The Woman of Shunem

The Faithful Hostess

As one who will later give up her home and become a refugee among foe Philistines for seven years and who will go directly to foe king to have her home and land restored (2 Kings 8:1–6), clearly foe Shunammite is no "lightweight." She can defend herself and can maintain her cause. She is obviously hurt, angry, and distressed, but she does not go all the way to Mount Carmel merely to criticize Elisha and to seek redress of her grievances; she makes this trip on behalf of her child.[1]

—Gene Rice

Scripture References

2 Kings 4, 8

Biography

The woman of Shunem lived during the period of Jehoram, king of Israel, which was around 850 BC. Her exact identity, for whatever reason, was not revealed by Elisha. However, we know from Scripture that she was a wealthy woman, prominent in her village, and was a faithful follower of God.

Elisha's journeys frequently took him through the village of Shunem, located in the land of the tribe of Issachar. Shunem also happened to be where the Philistines encamped when they came against King Saul, and where Abishag, the companion of King David in his old age, was from. Many times during his travels, Elisha was accompanied by his servant Gehazi.

This woman and her husband were familiar with the prophet Elisha and showed him hospitality during his travels. They even went so far as to construct a small room on their roof and made it available for Elisha's use whenever he was in Shunem. Because the passage focuses on the woman more than her husband—the woman may have been a more devout follower of God than her husband—there is no reason to believe he objected to the help she offered the prophet.

During one particular trip, Elisha and Gehazi were staying at the woman's house, and Elisha asked for the woman to come see him. Elisha instructed Gehazi to speak to the woman: "Say now to her, 'See, you have taken all this trouble for us; what is to be done for you? Would you have a word spoken on your behalf to the king or to the commander of the army?'" (2 Kings 4:13). The prophet was seeking a tangible way to say thank you for the hospitality that the woman and her husband had so graciously extended. He offered to speak to the king or commander of the army on her behalf, but she responded that she was content and did not want anything done for her.

Gehazi pointed out to Elisha later that the woman had no son and was married to an old man. This was significant because the woman would have no one to care for her after her husband died without a son to take over the family responsibilities. Elisha called the woman back and told her, "At this season, about this time next year, you shall embrace a son" (2 Kings 4:16). Not wanting to get her hopes up, the woman pleaded with Elisha not to lie to her, but the prophet's words proved true when she bore a son just as he had said.

When the woman's son had grown, he went to see his father in the field one day. Suddenly, he began to complain that his head hurt, so his father had him carried to his mother. The mother cradled her son on her lap, but around noon he died. The woman took her son and laid him on the bed of the prophet on the rooftop. Then she told her husband that she was taking a servant and a donkey to seek out Elisha, who was twenty-five miles away at Mount Carmel.

The prophet saw the woman approaching and sent Gehazi to meet her and inquire whether everything was well. Her response was merely, "All is well," and she continued on until finally reaching Elisha on the mountain. In her distress, the woman grabbed the prophet's feet and demanded answers: "Did I ask my lord for a son? Did I not say, 'Do not deceive me?'" (2 Kings 4:28).

Though the Lord had not revealed the tragedy to Elisha, by the woman's words he learned of the woman's bitter distress and swiftly sent Gehazi to run to the boy. Elisha gave the servant his staff and instructed him to hasten to the boy without stopping to speak to anyone. The woman made it clear that her faith was in God and in Elisha, and so she refused to return to her son without the prophet. Gehazi obeyed and went before Elisha and the woman, but nothing happened when he laid the staff on the child's face.

Not giving up hope, Elisha then went into the room and shut the door so he was alone with the boy. The prophet prayed to God and touched him, and life miraculously returned to the woman's son. Elisha instructed Gehazi to summon the Shunammite woman, and so she was reunited with her son.

Sometime after this miracle happened, Elisha spoke with the woman, "Arise, and depart with your household, and sojourn wherever you can, for the Lord has called for a famine, and it will come upon the land for seven years" (2 Kings 8:1). So the woman and her family dwelled in the land of the Philistines for seven years, and then after the famine was broken, they returned back to their home.

However, their return was not as simple as airing out a few rooms and cleaning all the cupboards in their home. The woman had to petition the king to obtain ownership of her house and land again. It just so happened that when she went before the king, Gehazi had just been telling him of how Elisha miraculously saved the life of the woman's son. Listening in amazement to both Gehazi and the woman recount the miraculous healing, the king decreed that the woman's house and land would be restored to her, along with the produce of the fields for the seven years they were gone.

Role in Redemption

Moxie is one of those fantastic words that do not get used enough. Dictionaries use words like *energy*, *courage*, *determination*, *vigor*, *verve*, and *know-how* to define it. It is a purely American word, but readers of 2 Kings can surely be forgiven for seeing the living definition of it in the woman of Shunem described in chapters 4 and 8 of that book.

We know a lot about this woman. We know her socioeconomic status; she was wealthy. We know her marital status; she was married. We know her place of residence was Shunem. By her attention and care of Elisha, we know she possessed a strong commitment to her faith. Yet we are never told her name.

Energy. She begins by taking the initiative to feed the prophet on his travels through her city. Next, she approaches her husband about constructing a special room so that they can host the prophet and his servant on their journeys.

Know-how. This woman of Shunem does not seem to be without a plan. She has a room constructed to her specifications, she outfits it just the way she envisions it needs to be. Later, when her son tragically falls and dies a swift death, she seems to know exactly what to do. She acts urgently and decisively. She gently lays her dead son on the prophet's bed. She knows what mount she needs, and she travels at great speed to see the prophet, stopping for no one, including Elisha's own servant.

Courage. Elisha is not condemned in this passage by God, but the woman of Shunem certainly has some pointed words for the prophet. Now, we would all hope that the prophet would see the grief of a woman who just lost her son, but what she says seems to be far different than merely a mother's grief. She rebukes the prophet and accuses him of deceit. Grieving or not, this was a serious accusation, particularly when you consider that just a couple of chapters earlier, in 2 Kings, two bears emerged from the forest and mutilated forty-two young boys who had mocked Elisha for being bald. It took significant courage for this woman to reproach the prophet. We would do well to notice that the passage does not condemn Elisha, but neither does it condemn the woman for her strong words.

Vigor. Essentially, this woman functioned as the general contractor for Elisha's room at her house. Later, when her son died, this woman rode a donkey as fast as she could on a twenty-mile trek to see the prophet. Then she immediately turned around and made the trip all over again. Later, at the instruction of the prophet, she packed up her not-insignificant household and moved to the land of the Philistines for seven years before returning.

Again and again, we see in this woman's brief story something stirring within her. She is not someone willing to stand aside and watch the world go by. She knows what is right, she knows what needs to be done, and she puts everything that she has into doing those things. Despite all of this, she endures significant adversity. The death of her son and the loss of her family's assuredly expansive home and property show her, the prophet, and the modern reader that God is willing to allow even those who boldly and vigorously do what is right to endure calamity and misfortune. Yet we see something rare when the Shunammite woman is faced with disaster. When life hands this woman a bitter pill, she shows no hesitation while believing that God can, and possibly will, rectify the situation. When her son dies, only once before in all of human history has a resurrection occurred. But that fact does not stop her, nor does it seem to slow her down in her quest to beseech the prophet to intercede on her behalf.

It is a shame that the Shunammite woman is all but forgotten today. We often speak of how God sovereignly rewards great faith, and that is most certainly true. Yet we rarely speak of how God sovereignly rewards great moxie. This woman's spirit is all the proof we need.

By the Numbers

Children had by the woman of Shunem: 1

Miles from Shunem to Mount Carmel, Elisha's home: 20

Years the woman of Shunem lived in the land of the Philistines at Elisha's direction: 7

Things We Wondered

Why did Elisha speak through his servant to the Shunammite woman instead of speaking to her directly?

Why did Elisha think the woman needed a word spoken on her behalf to the king or commander of the army?

Why did the Shunnamite woman conceal her son's death from her husband, and then later tell Gehazi that all was well?

14

Esther

The Queen

> The Esther story is an example of how at one crucial moment in history the covenant promises God had made were fulfilled, not by his miraculous intervention, but through completely ordinary events.[1]
>
> —Karen H. Jobes

Scripture References

Esther 1–10

Biography

The book about Esther takes place during the reign of Ahasuerus, more popularly known as King Xerxes I. He reigned in Persia, made up of more than 127 provinces, from 486–465 BC. Esther was a beautiful and desirable woman, who was swept up in events not of her making or her choice but which were clearly authored by God.

During the third year of Xerxes' reign, in the winter capital of Susa, he hosted a magnificent 180-day-long feast for his servants and officials so he could show off his marvelous riches. This feast was naturally followed by a week-long banquet for all of the guests. The richness and grandeur of the décor, food, and drink at this banquet impressed all who attended. Indeed, the royal wine flowed freely and without restriction. Parallel to the king's feast, Queen Vashti also held a feast for the women in the palace.

On the seventh and last day of the banquet, Xerxes requested that Queen Vashti appear before him and his banquet attendees, so that her beauty could delight them all. In a bold move, Queen Vashti refused to come at the king's command. Although many guesses can be made, the Bible does not give Queen Vashti's reason for defying the king's wishes. Her refusal angered the king so greatly that he, after consulting his advisors, banished her from his presence and took away her crown. They feared that other women would see the precedent set by her defiance and would show contempt to their husbands as well. Xerxes sent out a royal order saying that Vashti would never again see the king, and that her royal position would be stripped from her and given to someone more deserving.

Sometime later, the king's anger subsided and he began to think about finding a replacement queen. Following the suggestion of his advisors, Xerxes appointed officers throughout all the provinces of his kingdom to find the most beautiful young virgins. They were kept under the charge of Hegai in the king's harem in Susa, where they underwent beauty treatments to prepare for the king.

One of the women chosen was a Jewish girl named Esther, also known by her Hebrew name *Hadassah*. Esther was raised by her cousin Mordecai because she did not have a father or mother. Both were Benjaminites, descended from Israelites who were taken captive when Nebuchadnezzar defeated Judah.

The impressive beauty of Esther led to her being placed in the king's harem. She quickly gained favor with Hegai, who gave her a portion of food and cosmetics and advanced her to the most prominent place in the harem. God provided for her safety and comfort through Hegai. Mordecai also looked after his cousin by checking on her daily, and instructing her not to reveal her Judean heritage.

According to his wishes, the king's women prepared themselves for a minimum of a year with beauty treatments. When it was Esther's turn to be presented to the king, she followed Hegai's advice, and so the king showed great favor and grace to her. Xerxes loved Esther so greatly that he made her queen and placed the royal crown on her head. To celebrate, the king hosted another great feast in honor of Esther.

A while later Mordecai overheard a plot by two of the king's eunuchs to overthrow Xerxes. He passed the information on to Esther, who in turn told the information to the king. The affair was investigated and the men found to be guilty, so they were both hanged as punishment. This event was recorded in Persian government documents, including Mordecai's role in thwarting the evil plot, and witnessed by the king.

Sometime after these things happened, Xerxes promoted a man named Haman to be his right-hand man over all the other officials in the kingdom. Everyone bowed down to Haman and showed deference for his new position—everyone except Mordecai, that is. This act of defiance greatly offended Haman, and so he set out to take revenge on all the Jews in the kingdom, for he discovered that Mordecai was a Jew.

Haman cast lots (also called Pur) to find the best time to approach the king with a plan to decimate the Jews. He promised to make a large contribution to the kingdom's treasuries if the king agreed to make a decree that all the Jews should be destroyed. Xerxes was convinced by Haman's logic that the Jews were scattered throughout the provinces and that they kept different laws from the king's laws, and so he approved of Haman's plan. The king did not even accept Haman's offer of money, which would have been two-thirds of the kingdom's yearly income, but ordered the annihilation of the Jewish people under Haman's supervision.

And so it was that an edict was sent out to each province, commanding the officials and governors to kill the Jews and plunder their possessions on the thirteenth day of the twelfth month, which is Adar. This decree, which was celebrated by Xerxes and Haman, created much confusion in Susa and immeasurable grief among the Jews in the whole kingdom. Mordecai responded with great mourning, fasting, and weeping.

Mordecai tried to visit Esther to tell her of the king's decree but was denied entrance because he had torn off his clothing and was wearing sackcloth and ashes. So Esther sent one of the eunuchs assigned to attend her to go and meet with Mordecai and find out what was wrong. Returning with the grim details and a copy of the signed edict, Hathach the eunuch related everything Mordecai had said to Esther. He also told the queen that Mordecai had requested she visit the king and dissuade him from executing Haman's evil plot against the Jews. Esther was afraid because she knew the king could execute her for approaching him without first being summoned. She finally relented and agreed to approach the king.

First, she requested that Mordecai and all the Jews fast and pray on her behalf for three days and nights as she prepared to approach the king. On the third day, Esther dressed carefully in her royal robes and stood in the inner court until the king took notice of her. When he did spot her waiting, he extended the golden scepter in a gesture of approval. She humbly requested the presence of Xerxes and Haman at a lavish banquet she had prepared for them. As they were drinking wine at the end of the feast, Xerxes granted to Esther anything she wanted, even up to half his kingdom. Rather than reveal her true desire to rescue her people, she again requested the presence of the two men at a feast the following day.

Lulled into a false sense of security, Haman left the feast elated with his newfound popularity. This contentment was short-lived, however, as he encountered Mordecai in the king's gate. Mordecai did not afford Haman the same esteem as did his niece, and so Haman went home full of rage and vengeful thoughts. Along with his wife and friends, Haman devised a plan to retaliate against Mordecai by building a gallows and having Mordecai hung from it.

Unbeknownst to Haman, Xerxes had been unable to sleep that night and so ordered his servants to read from the government documents. While listening, he remembered the events whereby Mordecai helped to thwart an overthrow of the kingdom by two of the king's eunuchs. The king realized that Mordecai had never been rewarded for his honorable service and the next morning asked Haman, "What should be done to the man whom the king delights to honor?" (Esther 6:6). Haman was puffed up in his own mind and assumed that the king spoke of honoring him. He replied that the man should be given royal robes and the king's own horse to ride, and that he should be paraded through the city so all would see the honor bestowed upon him.

What delicious irony! Haman had come to the court to gain the king's approval for having Mordecai executed, but instead had unwittingly placed the very honor and esteem he craved for himself upon his enemy's head. Not surprisingly, Haman returned home in mortification where he received nothing but discouragement and pessimism from his wife and friends.

Even though Haman was overcome with despair, the king's eunuchs soon arrived and escorted him to the queen's feast. It was during this second feast that Xerxes again asked Esther what she wanted, and pledged that he would give her whatever she wanted, up to half of his kingdom. This time, Esther made known her true desire and asked the king to save her people from the enemy who plotted against them. Xerxes was astounded that anyone would plot against the people of his beautiful Queen Esther, and he demanded to know who would do such a thing. Esther clearly asserted, "A foe and enemy! This wicked Haman!" (Esther 7:6).

Xerxes was full of wrath for the man who had plotted against the Jews, and before the night was over he gave orders that Haman be hung from the very gallows he had built for Mordecai. The king also bestowed Haman's estate upon Esther, who gave it over to Mordecai. He also rescinded Haman's evil decree that the Jews be destroyed, and allowed them to defend themselves against attacks from their enemies. God made a way for the Jews to gain the victory over their enemies. The king granted one final request to Queen Esther, who asked that the ten sons of Haman also be hung from the gallows.

From the two days of rescue and salvation granted to the Jews by Xerxes and Queen Esther came the Jewish holiday of Purim. Esther 9:20–22 describes it this way:

> And Mordecai recorded these things and sent letters to all the Jews who were in all the provinces of King Ahasuerus, both near and far, obliging them to keep the fourteenth day of the month Adar and also the fifteenth day of the same, year by year, as the days on which the Jews got relief from their enemies, and as the month that had been turned for them from sorrow into

> gladness and from mourning into a holiday; that they should make them days of feasting and gladness, days for sending gifts of food to one another and gifts to the poor.

The canonicity of the book of Esther has been the center of many theological debates. Many theologians claim that it should not be included in the Bible because it does not mention the name of God. However, the book and the woman after whom it is named showed great faith in God during a tumultuous and terrifying time.

Role in Redemption

Skeptics of the Bible will make the claim that the Bible is a sexist book, and in particular the Old Testament. They will suggest that men such as Moses, David, and Elijah were prominent and central to the Old Testament's story, while women were relegated to the shadows. This perceived imbalance is evidence to some that the pages of the Scriptures are tainted at best and fraudulent at worst. The alleged sexism of the Old Testament is considered proof positive that for women Christianity is institutionalized oppression.

There are many problems with this view of femininity in the Bible, not the least of which is that it ignores the truth of the contributions of many of these women. Esther is the perfect example. It is hard to find someone more important to the Jewish faith and by extension the Christian faith than Esther. Without Esther, Judaism would not exist, and Jews would not exist.

Moses was the lawgiver, David was the monarch who all other monarchs descend from and are compared to, and Elijah was the boldest of the prophets who called the people back to God, but without Esther, none of that matters. If the Jewish people had been exterminated, the Law would have been irrelevant. If the plans of Haman to destroy the remnants of the nation of Judah had come to fruition, there would never have been another king to compare to King David. If Queen Esther stood by while her people were slaughtered, the tales of Elijah's defiance of wicked kings and queens would long ago have drifted from memory.

One of the Old Testament's greatest heroes is a woman. Perhaps the reason why the Old Testament is considered to have a problem with women, despite the story of Esther, is really more about the New Testament. You might think that Esther would garner a lot of attention in the New Testament, that surely significant pieces of theology would be derived from her story of courage and willingness to sacrifice. This, however, is not the case. Esther is nonexistent in the New Testament. And as powerful as her story is, as much as it has to teach us about God's sovereignty, none of the New Testament authors quote from the book that bears the queen's name, or even refer to Esther.

Where would God's plan of redemption have been without Esther? We have a good clue in Esther 4, when Mordecai tells Esther,

> Do not think to yourself that in the king's palace you will escape any more than all the other Jews. For if you keep silent at this time, relief and deliverance will rise for the Jews from another place, but you and your father's house will perish. And who knows whether you have not come to the kingdom for such a time as this?
>
> Esther 4: 13–15

Esther was an orphaned girl raised by her cousin in a foreign land. She was surrounded by a people and a culture that were hostile to her, her ethnicity, and her religion. She was certainly no one's pick to be the heroine that her people needed. In Mordecai's words, we see the truth of the dangerous situation in which Esther and the Jews found themselves. They were desperately in need of salvation, and God would save them. Esther was God's chosen method of bringing about the salvation of His people. God did not have to use Esther, and she could have chosen to only try to save herself, but she chose to be the one whom God used to save His people. Esther chose to be the one who saved the day; she chose to be the one who made everything after her possible.

By the Numbers

Length of days of the feast thrown by King Ahasuerus in Esther 1: 180

Length of days of the banquet held at the end of the 180-day feast: 7

Height in cubits of the gallows intended for Mordecai that was actually used for Haman: 50

Number of Haman's sons also hanged: 10

Number of enemies of the Jews killed: 75,000

Things We Wondered

Why did Vashti refuse Xerxes' summons?

What exactly was involved in pleasing Xerxes to be chosen as queen?

Why did Esther have multiple banquets before presenting her true request to Xerxes?

15

Gomer

The Harlot

But the wife of the prophet became an adulteress. What shame, what public disgrace, what burning anguish to the sensitive heart of the prophet! . . . To what depths this led Gomer is clear from the price to be paid for her redemption. Fifteen pieces of silver. The price of a common slave was thirty pieces of silver, according to Exodus 21:32. She had lowered herself to such a plane where she was worth but half the price of a common slave. The homer and lethech of barley speak of her utter worthlessness, for this was the food of animals. Nothing so undoes man altogether and ruins him completely as defection from the Lord. It is no less than high treason against high heaven.[1]

—Charles L. Feinberg

Scripture References

Hosea 1–3

Biography

God used the life of Gomer to draw an astonishing parallel between a prostitute and the people of Israel. The harlotry she practiced was the same as the unfaithfulness of God's people when they turned to idol worship. Yet despite the hurt and damage caused by sin, God and His prophet Hosea remained steadfast in their love.

The book of Hosea was written during the reign of the Israelite king Jeroboam. God spoke to His prophet Hosea and told him, "Go, take to yourself a wife of whoredom and have children of whoredom, for the land commits great whoredom by forsaking the Lord" (Hosea 1:2). There has been much debate regarding whether Gomer was already a prostitute, or if she turned to prostitution after she was married to Hosea. Because telling Hosea to marry a prostitute would have presented a moral discrepancy that disobeyed the Law, the better option seems to be that God was telling Hosea what would happen in the future.

God also foretold that Gomer would bear children. First, she gave birth to a son, whom the Lord told them to name Jezreel. This name means "God sows" and was given to their son because God intended to punish the house of Jehu for the blood shed at Jezreel. Next, she bore a daughter, and God told them to name her Lo-Ruhamah. This name means "no mercy," because God would not have mercy on the kingdom of Israel. Last, Gomer gave birth to another son, whom they named Lo-Ammi. This name means "not my people" and was given by God because the Israelites had forsaken God.

In Hosea 2, we see a prophetic message that began by describing the relationship between Hosea and Gomer but ultimately portrayed the relationship of Israel with God. Hosea pleaded with his children to intercede with their mother and convince her to turn from her harlotry. He explained the consequences if she refused to repent—that she would be exposed, barren, and that her children born from adultery would not receive mercy.

Despite Gomer's repeated acts of adultery, Hosea remained faithful to her and pursued her as he was directed by the Lord. In Hosea 3:1, the Lord said to the prophet, "Go again, love a woman who is loved by another man and is an adulteress, even as the Lord loves the children of Israel, though they turn to other gods and love cakes of raisins."

At some point, because of her sinful choices, Gomer had somehow been sold to someone as a slave or servant, because Hosea had to purchase her freedom with fifteen shekels of silver and a homer and a half of barley. One commentator summarized this price this way:

> Fifteen shekels of silver was half the price of a dead slave (Exodus 21:32), and barley was cattle food. A homer and a half cost about fifteen shekels of silver. So Hosea evidently paid the price of a dead slave for his wife. She was not regarded as worth much.[2]

Gomer is not mentioned again in Hosea or anywhere else in the Bible, but presumably she stayed with Hosea. God's purpose in calling Hosea to a harlot wife and children was to give the prophet firsthand knowledge of the anguish and suffering He experienced in loving an unfaithful people.

Role in Redemption

One of the most iconic photographs ever captured on film was taken by photographer Alfred Eisenstaedt on August 14, 1945, at 5:52 p.m. in New York City's Times Square. That day marked the end of World War II, and Eisenstaedt went to Times Square to capture the spontaneous celebrations that broke out as people learned that four years of war were finally over. He took many photos that day, but the one that everyone remembers is of a sailor, in his dress blue uniform, giving a nurse, dressed all in white, a whale of a kiss. The sailor is dipping the nurse as he kisses her, and the photo looks like two lovers embracing at the end of a romantic dance. That singular picture became so iconic because in one frame it captured the mood of an entire nation. The end of the war brought relief, joy, and a clear lack of inhibition. The feelings and emotions of hundreds of millions of people in one moment were captured in one photograph.

In many ways, Gomer is God's redemptive iconic photograph. Unlike many of the other women whose stories appear in the Bible, she is largely two-dimensional. We know nothing about her background or about her motivations. There are really only three things we can say for sure about Gomer: the depth of her depravity, the lengths to which her husband was willing to go to bring her back, and the theological truth that her story teaches.

Unlike other women who had great moral failings, we see nothing in Gomer to balance the scales in our opinion of her. She was a mother who left her husband and children for prostitution, and whose wayward path took her into slavery. There is little to love about Gomer. Nothing we see about her in the book of Hosea commends her to us. And as much as we might not want to admit it, this is our exact state before God as well. The depravity that we see displayed in the life of Gomer is present in us all. Gomer's sinfulness was displayed on a marquee for all to see. Most of us do a better job of concealing our depravity, but in reality we are as dark and in need of rescue as Gomer, enslaved by her own sins.

The book of Hosea makes it very clear that Gomer's rabid pursuit of debauchery was an illustration of the nation of Israel's own unfaithfulness to God, and she is the ultimate example not only of our true state, but also of the lengths to which God is willing to go to redeem people who are unfaithful to Him.

Gomer's story is everyone's story. She exists in the Bible as a picture not of how low a person can sink, but of how far God is willing to go to redeem those in need of redemption.

By the Numbers

Children had by Gomer: 3

Pieces of silver Hosea paid to buy Gomer out of slavery: 30

Things We Wondered

Was Gomer a prostitute before she married Hosea, or did she enter prostitution after her marriage?

What became of their marriage after Hosea bought Gomer back from slavery?

Why did Gomer choose to become a prostitute when she had the love of a faithful husband like Hosea?

16

Mary, Mother of Jesus

Mother of the Messiah

> The tender Mother of Christ does the same here, and teaches us, with her words and by the example of her experience, how to know, love and praise God. For since she boasts, with heart leaping for joy and praising God, that He regarded her despite her low estate and nothingness.[1]
>
> —Martin Luther

Scripture References

Matthew 1, 2, 13; Mark 3, 6; Luke 1, 2; John 2, 19; Acts 1

Biography

There are two genealogies of Jesus in the Gospels, one in Matthew and one in Luke. While it is not possible to be certain, there is good reason to believe that the genealogy in Luke is that of Jesus through Mary. If that is the case, it would mean that her ancestors were from the tribes of Judah and Levi. We know from John 19:25 that she had a sister, but little else is known of her family other than that she was a relative of Elizabeth, the mother of John the Baptist.

When we first encounter her in the Gospels, Mary lived in the city of Nazareth, in the region of Galilee, and was betrothed to a man named Joseph. In that culture, the betrothal and the marriage that would come after it would have been arranged by her parents. The Bible does not tell us how old she was at this time, but she could have been betrothed as early as twelve, usually no older than eighteen.

Six months after her relative Elizabeth became pregnant, the angel Gabriel appeared to Mary. The angel greeted her, saying, "Greetings, favored one! The Lord is with you" (Luke 1:28 NASB). This greeting bewildered Mary, but Gabriel urged her not to be afraid. She was to bear a son named Jesus. Gabriel said four things about Jesus that mimic God's promise to David in 2 Samuel 7: He would be great and He would be called the Son of the Most High, the Lord God would give Him the throne of His father David, He would reign over the house of Jacob forever, and His kingdom would have no end.

Mary asked Gabriel how this would happen since she was a virgin. He told her, "The Holy Spirit will come upon you, and the power of the Most High will overshadow you. Therefore the child to be born will be holy; he will be called the Son of God" (Luke 1:35 NET). Gabriel told Mary that her formerly barren relative Elizabeth had also conceived. Nothing was impossible with God. Mary responded that she was the servant of the Lord, and may it be done to her according to Gabriel's words.

After Gabriel's visit, Mary went to see her pregnant relative Elizabeth at her home in the hill country. When Elizabeth heard

Mary's voice, Elizabeth's child, John the Baptist, leapt in her womb. She cried with a loud voice,

> Blessed are you among women, and blessed is the fruit of your womb! And how has it happened to me, that the mother of my Lord would come to me? For behold, when the sound of your greeting reached my ears, the baby leaped in my womb for joy. And blessed is she who believed that there would be a fulfillment of what had been spoken to her by the Lord.
>
> Luke 1:42–45 NASB

Mary responded to Elizabeth with a poem or song that has become known as her Magnificat. The term *Magnificat* is from the Latin for "exalts" or "glorifies." Mary's song parallels Hannah's similar monologue in 1 Samuel 2. The Magnificat is a song of immense praise to God for His greatness. Mary stayed with Elizabeth for three months.

After Mary returned to Nazareth, it was discovered that she was pregnant. Joseph believed that Mary had been unfaithful to him and intended to quietly divorce her, something legally required in a Jewish betrothal. In such circumstances, Joseph could choose to break the betrothal publicly, which would declare Mary's assumed sin to all, or he could simply hand her a certificate of divorce in front of two witnesses. Based on the belief that Mary had been promiscuous, he chose to break from her, but to do so without publicly shaming her. In the face of what he believed to be intense personal betrayal, Joseph evidenced both a concern for righteousness and compassion.

In a dream, an angel (possibly Gabriel) appeared to Joseph and told him to take Mary as his wife because the child was conceived by the Holy Spirit. The angel said that Mary would have a son named Jesus and He would save His people from their sins. The angel's words were a fulfillment of Isaiah 7:14.

Joseph did what the angel commanded and married Mary, but he did not have sexual relations with her until after she gave birth to Jesus.

Sometime after the angel appeared to Joseph, the Roman emperor, Caesar Augustus, ordered everyone in the Roman Empire to go to their ancestral hometown for a census. Caesar's decree meant that Joseph would need to travel to Bethlehem because he was a descendant of King David. It is a little unclear if Mary and Joseph were married by this time or not, but even as a betrothed couple it would have been necessary for her to accompany him. Due to the influx of people traveling for the census, there was nowhere to stay in Bethlehem. Soon Mary went into labor and gave birth to her son in the only space they could find—a stable. He was wrapped and placed in a manger. Surrounded by cattle, in an unfamiliar village, Mary began motherhood to the Savior of the world.

In a nearby field, an angel appeared to a group of shepherds who were watching their flocks. The angel praised God and said that the Messiah had been born in Bethlehem. After the angel left, the shepherds went to Bethlehem to find Mary, Joseph, and the baby and told them about the visit of the angel. According to Luke, "But Mary treasured up all these things and pondered them in her heart. The shepherds returned, glorifying and praising God for all the things they had heard and seen, which were just as they had been told" (Luke 2:19–20 NIV).

After Jesus' birth, He was taken to the temple in Jerusalem. There, a man named Simeon met them and told Mary,

> Behold, this Child is destined for the fall and rising of many in Israel, and for a sign which will be spoken against (yes, a sword will pierce through your own soul also), that the thoughts of many hearts may be revealed.
>
> Luke 2:34–35 NKJV

Sometime after the birth of Jesus, Magi from the East came to visit the family in Bethlehem. The wise men were "non-Jewish religious astrologers who, from astronomical observations, inferred the birth of a great Jewish king."[2] Ever since Jesus had been born they had been tracking a star in the sky that they believed declared His birth. The Magi brought gifts of gold, frankincense, and myrrh. God warned them in a dream to avoid King Herod on their way home, so they departed a different way. After the Magi left, an angel appeared to Joseph in a dream, telling him, "Get up! Take the Child and His mother and flee to Egypt, and remain there until I tell you; for Herod is going to search for the Child to destroy Him" (Matthew 2:13 NASB). They obeyed the angel and lived in Egypt for a number of years (as many as ten) until they returned to Nazareth.

At the age of twelve, Jesus was separated from Mary and Joseph on their return from Passover in Jerusalem. After three days of searching for Him, they found Him in the temple lecturing the teachers, and Mary said to Jesus,

> "Son, why have You treated us like this? Your father and I have been anxiously searching for You."
>
> "Why were you searching for Me?" He asked them. "Didn't you know that I had to be in My Father's house?"
>
> Luke 2:48–49 HCSB

At the end of this exchange, Luke tells us again that Mary "Kept all these things in her heart." Aside from references to his alleged parentage of Jesus, this is also the last mention of Joseph in the Bible. No mention is made of what may have happened to him, but by the time of Jesus' crucifixion it is clear that he is not in the picture. Most scholars have attributed his disappearance from the story to death.

We know nothing of the years of Mary's life between the incident with Jesus in the temple and the beginning of Jesus' public ministry. A number of passages in the Gospels refer to Jesus having brothers and sisters. The obvious conclusion is that after the birth of Jesus, Mary and Joseph consummated their marriage like any other married couple. The rest of what we know of Mary comes from brief snapshots in the Gospels and in Acts.

Jesus' first miracle, turning water into wine at a wedding in Cana, was performed at the urging of Mary. Sometime into His public ministry some of Jesus' family thought He had lost His mind. Among those who came to speak with Him were Mary and Jesus' brothers, but He did not grant them an audience. Mary was present at the crucifixion, and while Jesus was dying, He asked His disciple John to care for His mother. In the book of Acts, Mary was present at the beginning of the church in the upper room on Mount Olive. From there she leaves the pages of the biblical record.

Church tradition has Mary following the apostle John to the city of Ephesus and finishing her life serving the church in that city. The city of Ephesus has ruins of a first-century home that are marketed as the house of the Virgin Mary. Many historians are dubious of this claim as it is based on a nineteenth-century nun's alleged vision of the house. Even without reliable facts to go on regarding her possible time in Ephesus, we know more about Mary than we do almost anyone else in the New Testament.

Role in Redemption

Mary is the Christmas tree of biblical women. For most of the year, at least in Protestant churches, Mary is all but invisible. Then December rolls around, and she suddenly emerges as the subject of sermons, songs, paintings, and nativity sets everywhere. Pastors expound her virtues, musicians celebrate her, and little girls portray her in countless plays. After a month-long turn in the spotlight, advent season ends, and before you know it, Mary is once again relegated to the theological attic for the next eleven months.

The paucity of teaching on Mary is probably a reaction to the Roman Catholic Church's teachings on Mary, which have been rejected by Protestantism. If there is one thing for which Protestantism has shined throughout its history, it is protesting, and in some respects the absence of Mary from the church is probably an unintentional counterbalance to the Catholic teachings that Mary was herself sinless and a mediator between mankind and God. In rejecting Catholicism's erroneous teachings, it can at times feel like the person of Mary has been rejected as well.

Mary's yearly disappearing act really is quite a shame. The New Testament contains more information about Mary than all but a handful of people. One theologian has suggested that the only people we read more biographical information about in the New Testament than Mary are Jesus, Paul, Peter, and John.[3] With this wealth of information, you would expect Mary to be prevalent in churches, but unless the sounds of Christmas carols are echoing through the halls, you probably hear nothing about the woman who was and is integral to the Christian faith.

Just how important is Mary? Well, she was the mother of the Messiah, which is surely something not to be taken lightly. When God came to the earth to dwell among His creation, He chose Mary as the one to carry both God and man in her womb. To call this a privilege is to understate the issue vividly. Of all the women in the world, Mary was handpicked by the Almighty to raise the Son of God. Let the enormity of Mary's reality sink in. In a moment she went from a simple, small-town girl to an unwed, expectant mother who was carrying the Savior that God had promised thousands of years earlier.

Mary's role as the mother of the Christ is worth every sermon that it inspires, but there is a depth to Mary we frequently miss in our yearly nativity flybys. Mary's contributions to the Christian faith were extensive. One often-overlooked role that Mary played for the followers of Jesus was that of trailblazer. When she was visited by an angelic messenger, and she believed his message, Mary was in fact the first to believe in Jesus. Her faith preexisted that of Peter, John, and the apostles. As one commentator put it,

> It is no exaggeration to say that for Luke, Mary has heard the gospel of Jesus Christ, and indeed is the first one to have done so. . . . When in the annunciation Luke reports Mary's answer, "Let it be done to me according to your word," he is describing not only one who is consenting to be the physical mother of Jesus but also and very importantly one who meets Jesus' criterion for his family of disciples, indeed the first one.[4]

Every person who has come to faith in Christ is following in the footsteps of two thousand years of Christians of every shape, size, ethnicity, race, and nationality imaginable. Placing faith in Christ is a road to redemption that is well-worn from those who came before us. Kings, prophets, apostles, martyrs, lepers, and every strata of mankind have trod this path. But we would do well to remember the first steps on this trail were faith in God's promise of redemption exercised by a young teenage girl.

By the Numbers

Months into Elizabeth's pregnancy when the angel Gabriel came to Mary: 6

Months Mary stayed with Elizabeth: 3

Age range for when Mary would have been betrothed to Joseph: 12 to 18

Things We Wondered

How old was Mary when she became pregnant with Jesus?

What happened to Joseph?

What was it like to raise the perfect child?

17

Elizabeth

The Mother of the Forerunner

> Little is said in Scripture about Elisabeth. She sang the first song of the New Testament, and when you have a soloist like this, you should not ignore her. She is a remarkable person. She had faith while her husband Zacharias did not. He was struck dumb because of his unbelief, but Elisabeth was not. She believed God.[1]
>
> —J. Vernon McGee

Scripture References

Luke 1

Biography

Elizabeth was not only the wife of a righteous man, but she was praised for being righteous as well. Her husband, Zechariah (referred to as Zacharias in some translations), was a priest, and she herself descended from the Aaronic tribe of priests. Together they "were both righteous before God, walking blamelessly in all the commandments and statutes of the Lord" (Luke 1:6).

Despite their faithful obedience to God, Elizabeth and Zechariah were yet barren in their advanced years. In the times in which they lived, during the days of King Herod, a woman's barrenness was often seen as a punishment or withholding of blessing from God. If a woman did not have children, she had no security for her future should something happen to her husband. However, it is clear, as we will see later in her story, that God had a plan to bless Elizabeth all along.

As part of his priestly duties, Zechariah would twice yearly serve at the temple of the Lord for a week. While the priest was inside the temple burning incense for the Lord, the people gathered outside to pray. It was during one of these times of service that Zechariah was chosen by lot to burn incense inside the holy of holies, and this moment forever changed his life. While in the innermost part of the temple, he encountered an angel who told him,

> Do not be afraid, Zechariah, for your prayer has been heard, and your wife Elizabeth will bear you a son, and you shall call his name John. And you will have joy and gladness, and many will rejoice at his birth, for he will be great before the Lord.
>
> Luke 1:13–15

The angel Gabriel went on to say that John would be used by God as a forerunner for the coming Messiah. Empowered by the Holy Spirit, John would prepare the hearts of the people to receive their promised Savior by turning many of them back to God.

The angel brought news that Zechariah had longed to hear for many years, but he still found it incredible to imagine. The priest asked the angel how he would actually know this message to be true, and Gabriel said that Zechariah would be unable to speak until the day of the baby's birth because of his unbelief.

While Zechariah spoke with the angel inside the holy of holies, the people outside the temple began to get nervous. Had God struck the priest dead for some sin in his life? Imagine their astonishment and confusion when he finally emerged from the temple unscathed but for the inability to speak! Nonetheless, the people realized that Zechariah had seen a vision while in the temple. He tried to communicate with signs, but no matter how much he tried to speak, he remained mute. When his service was completed, he went home to Elizabeth and she conceived.

The Bible says, "For five months she kept herself hidden, saying, 'Thus the Lord has done for me in the days when he looked on me, to take away my reproach among people'" (Luke 1:24–25). There has been quite a bit of discussion as to why Elizabeth would hide herself away for the first five months of her pregnancy, which might suggest that she was ashamed or embarrassed. However, it seems more logical that secluding herself for the first five months of the pregnancy might be a way of protecting her health and the health of her baby since she was an older woman.[2]

In the sixth month of Elizabeth's pregnancy, Gabriel also visited her relative Mary and gave the news that she would also bear a son, the promised Messiah. Mary went at once to visit Zechariah and Elizabeth in the hill country. Upon hearing Mary's greeting, the baby leaped inside Elizabeth's womb, as if he already recognized the presence of his Messiah. Elizabeth was immediately filled with the Holy Spirit, and she too rejoiced at the arrival of Mary, the mother of her Lord.

Elizabeth gave birth to a healthy baby boy, and his arrival was met with much rejoicing by family and friends. The people who celebrated with the happy couple assumed that the new parents would name their son Zechariah after his father and wrote as such on a tablet for Zechariah to confirm. The fact that the well-wishers were also writing on a tablet—and not just Zechariah hearing their question and responding in writing—has led to some speculation on whether Zechariah was not only mute but deaf as well after encountering the angel. However, Zechariah corroborated what Elizabeth had already declared. The boy would be called John. It was this affirmation of John's name that showed his obedience and trust in God's plan for their son, and which prompted God to remove Zechariah's temporary disability. As soon as his speech returned, Zechariah blessed God, but the people were amazed and frightened.

John the Baptist fulfilled the angel's words, and he prepared the people to receive their beloved Messiah. Elizabeth showed great courage and faithfulness in her obedience to God, and was used mightily in God's plan of redemption.

Role in Redemption

Luke 1 gives us the story of Elizabeth, at least as much as the Bible record shows. What it does not give us would have been fascinating to see. Imagine if you will for a moment a woman in her home village waiting for her husband to return from a work trip. He returns mute, and possibly even deaf. The woman is incredibly confused by this bizarre turn of events until her husband, communicating by writing on a tablet, tells her that while he was away an angel of God appeared to him. The angel told him that his prayer had been heard and that he and his wife, despite being past normal child-bearing age, would conceive and give birth to a son. Their son would be a great man before God and they were to name him John. When the man doubted the angel's words, the angel declared that he would be unable to speak until these things came to pass.

How surreal it must have been to be that woman whose husband returned home communicating through sign language and hastily written notes of angels speaking and long-abandoned dreams of a son. How ludicrous life must have been for Elizabeth in those moments.

Of course, the scene between Zechariah and Elizabeth is not recorded in Scripture. And that is probably for the best, because it is so much more delightful to imagine that conversation taking place. Communication in marriage can be immensely difficult when both of you are able to speak, but every married couple can imagine how this conversation played out with Zechariah wildly gesticulating and writing as fast as possible, while a confounded Elizabeth struggled to grasp what exactly was going on.

We get a fantastic glimpse into the soul of Elizabeth in Luke 1:25, when she says, "This is the way the Lord has dealt with me in the days when He looked with favor upon me, to take away my disgrace among men" (NASB). Though in many ways by this point in her life Elizabeth seemed to have come to terms with her infertility (compare the impression she creates with that of Hannah in 1 Samuel, for example), God's work in her life in this way removed a terrible stigma. To be a woman in her time not having borne a child was embarrassing at best and at worst a sign of God's disfavor. When God promised her a son, all of that was taken away.

Through all of this, Elizabeth's perspective was perfectly clear. She was content to be the person God wanted her to be. She showed no jealousy of her relative, who was decades younger and who carried the One who would one day eclipse her own son. Elizabeth's son would live for the purpose of pointing the world to Mary's son, and she was content to be used by God in that capacity. As theologian Darrell Bock states with regard to Elizabeth, "Peace reigns among those who serve God as each understands his or her place in God's plan."[3]

When John was finally born, Zechariah was still unable to speak. Eight days later, when it came time to circumcise the boy, family and relatives were already calling the boy Zechariah.[4] With the boy's father unable to speak, it fell to Elizabeth to set the record straight. When she did declare that her son would be called John, the surrounding friends and family cared so little for her feelings and thoughts that they appealed to her mute husband for his opinion. By now, of course, Zechariah had learned his lesson, so when he wrote on a tablet that the child would be called John, his tongue was loosed.

Elizabeth seems to have been a woman without pretenses. When life dealt her a trying hand, she continued to be faithful. When God removed her disgrace, she continued to live out her faith in Him, trusting His plan. God brought forth a miracle in the life of Elizabeth, and the son that she raised would go on to be one of the greatest men history has ever known. Not only was God taking away Elizabeth's disgrace, but He was also filling her with the Holy Spirit. Though her pain had been real, it was also part of God's plan.

By the Numbers

Children given by God to Elizabeth: 1

Miles between Hebron and Jerusalem: 19

Number of times per year Zechariah served at the temple: 2

Number of months Elizabeth hid herself once she was pregnant: 5

Things We Wondered

What was Elizabeth's reaction when Zechariah came home unable to speak after his temple service?

Was Zechariah rendered mute, or mute and deaf after his encounter with the angel?

What exactly was Elizabeth's purpose while hiding herself during the first five months of her pregnancy?

How old was Elizabeth when she gave birth to John?

18

Anna

The Prophetess

> Some there were in Jerusalem that looked for redemption; yet but a few, for Anna, it should seem, had acquaintance with all of them that were joint-expectants with her of the Messiah; she knew where to find them, or they where to find her, and she told them all the good news, that she had seen the Lord; and it was great news, this of his birth now, as afterwards that of his resurrection.[1]
>
> —Matthew Henry

Scripture References

Luke 2

Biography

The story of Anna begins with Jesus' parents bringing Him to the temple not long after He was born. They went to offer the required sacrifice and to consecrate Him before the Lord. It was during their visit to the temple that Joseph and Mary met a prophetess named Anna.

Anna was the daughter of Phanuel from the tribe of Asher. The Bible describes her as "advanced in years, having lived with her husband seven years from when she was a virgin, and then as a widow until she was eighty-four" (Luke 2:36–37). There is some discussion among theologians as to her age because the text can actually mean she was eighty-four years old, or that she had been widowed for eighty-four years, which would place her age a bit over the 100-year mark. Either way, the author definitely intended to make known that Anna was an older woman, and as such was a figure of wisdom and maturity in the community.

Rather than remarry, which would afford her the social and financial security women needed at that time, she chose to remain single. Anna devoted her life to serving the Lord in the temple. Luke 2:37–38 says,

> She did not depart from the temple, worshiping with fasting and prayer night and day. And coming up at that very hour she began to give thanks to God and to speak of him to all who were waiting for the redemption of Jerusalem.

As soon as she saw Jesus with Mary and Joseph, she knew that this was the prophesied Messiah. Anna immediately gave thanks and prophesied to the people in the temple about the newborn Jesus.

Role in Redemption

To say that Anna's time in the Bible is brief is a bit of an understatement. She appears in only three verses in the Bible, all in the gospel of Luke, and half of the small passage about her is focused on her advanced age. The point of Anna's story is not her age. She had lived a long, full life, especially in that time, but her age is a prism that allows us to see just how many ways God had worked in her life. Let's take a brief stroll through history to see exactly what Anna saw and experienced.

We do not know for sure the exact year of Jesus' birth, but many New Testament scholars who have investigated the chronology of the life of Christ, such as Harold Hoehner, suggest that Jesus was born sometime around 4 BC. If we use that as our starting point, we can see that Anna would have been born between 88 BC and 108 BC. No matter which date is accurate, the early part of Anna's life would have been spent in a land ruled by Alexander Janneus, who was a king and high priest. Janneus expanded his kingdom to encompass almost as much land as Solomon had ruled over hundreds of years before. Though the borders of the country were near their former glory, Anna's formative years would not have been pleasant. As a king, Janneus was cruel and vicious. He was vehemently opposed by the Pharisees, and his actions led to open rebellion and six years of civil war. When he finally emerged victorious, Janneus took revenge on his enemies by publicly crucifying some 800 leaders of the revolt near Jerusalem.

The historian Josephus suggested that the six years of war cost 50,000 people their lives.[2] After Janneus's death, the kingdom was ruled by his wife, Alexandra Salome. After Alexandra's death, her sons fought for control of the kingdom, and again warfare spilled out onto the streets of Jerusalem. Eventually one son, Aristobulus, controlled Jerusalem, while another son, Hyrcanus, laid siege to the holy city.

All of this would have transpired during the time that Anna married, became a widow, and began to serve in the temple. Eventually both brothers sent for help to the Roman General

Pompey. Pompey attacked Jerusalem and conquered the land. During the battle for Jerusalem, Pompey's troops killed some 12,000 Jews, among them a large number of priests at the temple compound. Pompey himself entered the holy of holies, desecrating it, though he took nothing from it, and the next day he ordered the temple cleansed and the sacrifices and worship restored.[3]

Eventually, the Romans set up a local government that would subject the area of Palestine to Roman rule. The first of these rulers was Antipater II. When he was poisoned and died, two of his sons, Phasael and Herod, were named joint rulers of the region by Roman General Mark Antony. A few years later, one of Aristobulus's sons escaped Roman custody and led a revolt that briefly conquered the region again. In the conquest, Phasael died (possibly through suicide, possibly through poisoning), and when the revolt was finally put down, Herod was named the ruler of Palestine.

Herod's rule was marked by bloodshed, paranoia, and suspicion. He put to death forty-five of the most prominent citizens of Jerusalem and took their property. He married a woman who was a descendant of the former king Alexander Janneus, but eventually he murdered her and her two sons over fears that they were working to overthrow him. He named someone to be high priest, but a year later, fearful of that man's power, he had him drowned in the bath at Jericho. Of particular interest to Anna would have been Herod's many building projects, which included the refurbishing and enlarging of the temple in Jerusalem. By the time the temple project was undertaken, Anna would have been well into her sixties, if not her eighties. At some point, these renovations included putting a golden eagle, representing a Roman sun god, over the temple door. Aghast at such a brazen act, a group of Jewish students tore down the golden monstrosity. Herod responded by having them burned alive. The world around her was on fire, and Anna continued to fast and pray night and day in the temple.

Anna did not live a life of ease. She endured great losses, and was surrounded by violence, danger, and peril for most of her days on this planet. Her countrymen fought a civil war around her; she was surrounded by the bodies of priests slain by the Romans. Her days were many, but they were precarious. Through all that she endured, Anna focused on something in the future—the coming of redemption.

Through God's grace, Anna survived widowhood, civil war, sieges, conquests, and occupation by the mighty Roman army. Surely Anna's life was one marked by scars and near-misses emotionally, spiritually, and physically. Her guiding light through it all was the expectation of the redemption of Jerusalem. She saw its dawning and she experienced the daybreak of that redemption for herself.

By the Numbers

Anna's husbands: 1

Years she was married: 7

Years she lived as a widow: 84

Things We Wondered

How old was Anna actually?

Why did Anna never remarry?

How did Anna support herself when "she did not depart from the temple, worshiping with fasting and prayer night and day"?

19

Mary Magdalene

The Witness

> It is worth recalling that the Synoptists, who mention several women at the tomb, agree in naming Mary Magdalene first. This probably reflects the early church's memory of the fact that she was the first person to see the resurrected Jesus. Her witness was not as greatly utilized in the primitive preaching as was that of, say, Peter, doubtless owing to the fact that a woman's evidence was not normally admissible in court. . . . The Evangelists have nevertheless taken pains to honour her, and thoughtful Christians will remember that God delights to choose what the world deems foolish to shame the wise, so that no one may boast before him.[1]
>
> —D. A. Carson

Scripture References

Matthew 27–28; Mark 15–16; Luke 8, 24; John 19–20

Biography

Mary Magdalene was a woman who was mentioned several times throughout the Gospels, but in truth, not much is known about her.

She first appears in Luke 8 as part of a group of women who accompanied Jesus on His travels throughout the cities and villages. *Magdalene* probably refers to her hometown of Magdala, which was on the west side of the Sea of Galilee. She, along with Joanna and Susanna and others, provided for Jesus and the disciples while they spread the good news of God's kingdom to all who would listen. Mary and the other women with whom she traveled were distinct because they "had been healed of evil spirits and infirmities" (Luke 8:2). Specifically, the passage says that seven demons were cast out of Mary Magdalene.

There are various traditions in church history that fill in the gaps of Mary Magdalene's personal history, including the belief that she had been a prostitute before repenting and following Jesus. Another belief held by some is that she was Jesus' wife or mistress. However, these are traditions and are not substantiated by any information found in the inspired canonical gospels.

When Jesus was crucified, there was a group of women who had followed Jesus from Galilee to minister to Him, and now watched from a distance as He died. Mary Magdalene was numbered among this group of women. It is noteworthy that most of Jesus' disciples, the men to whom He grew so close and loved so much, were not present at His trial or crucifixion. Mary Magdalene, along with Mary the mother of James and Joseph, was also present when Jesus was buried in the tomb of Joseph of Arimathea.

At dawn on the third day after Jesus' death, Mary Magdalene, accompanied by a group of other women, went to the tomb to anoint His body with spices. Imagine their astonishment and alarm when they arrived at the tomb and found the stone rolled away! John 20:2 describes Mary Magdalene's reaction:

> So she ran and went to Simon Peter and the other disciple, the one whom Jesus loved, and said to them, "They have taken the Lord out of the tomb, and we do not know where they have laid him."

The timeline of Easter morning is ambiguous with regard to who was where and when. A lot of this confusion is due to the various gospel writers emphasizing different characters for their own particular reasons. None of their vantage points contradict, but they do focus on different people and actions in the Easter story. What we do know is that Mary Magdalene and the women were at the tomb, where they encountered the angel who said,

> Do not be alarmed. You seek Jesus of Nazareth, who was crucified. He has risen; he is not here. See the place where they laid him. But go, tell his disciples and Peter that he is going before you to Galilee. There you will see him, just as he told you.
>
> Mark 16:6–7

The women were afraid and did nothing at first, but then Luke 24:8–9 says that they remembered the words of the angel and did as he commanded them. Together, Mary Magdalene and the other women told the disciples all that they had seen and heard.

Upon hearing the disturbing news relayed by Mary Magdalene and the other women, the disciples scoffed and did not believe what the women had told them. But Peter and John left the other disciples and ran to the tomb to see for themselves. Peter arrived first and stooped to look inside the tomb, but saw nothing but the linen cloths Jesus had been wrapped in lying on the stone shelf. John arrived next and witnessed the empty tomb as well. Peter's reaction is not recorded in this passage, but the Bible says that John saw the empty tomb and believed.

From the biblical accounts, we know that Mary returned to the tomb at some point, and possibly so did the other women who initially accompanied her. After Peter and John went back home, Mary Magdalene lingered at the tomb weeping. It was then that she saw two angels sitting where Jesus' body had lain. The angels asked why she was crying, and she explained that she was distraught because someone had taken Jesus' body and she did not know where they had laid Him. Turning around, she encountered a man that the audience knows to be Jesus, but who was unfamiliar to Mary. But as soon as Jesus spoke her name, she recognized her risen Lord! Jesus says, "Do not cling to me, for I have not yet ascended to the Father; but go to my brothers and say to them, 'I am ascending to my Father and your Father, to my God and your God'" (John 20:17).

Mary might have wanted to revel in the revelation of the risen Savior, but Jesus had an important task for her. She was the first to whom the resurrected Lord revealed himself, and He needed her to begin spreading the good news.

Mary Magdalene appears nowhere else in Scripture. Theologians have speculated whether there may be a deeper meaning behind Jesus' revealing himself first to a woman, but what we know for certain is that He revealed himself to one who showed unwavering faith and devotion. Despite the other disciples' falling away in fear when Jesus was arrested and crucified, she remained steadfast in her support of her Lord.

Role in Redemption

June Carter Cash, Anne Bancroft, Barbara Hershey, Debra Messing, and Monica Bellucci all have portrayed Mary Magdalene.

Aside from Mary the mother of Jesus, she is probably the woman in the Bible most portrayed by film and television. Popular culture's fascination is a bit surprising. If all you do is read the scriptural accounts, Mary was notable in that she was the first witness to the resurrection, but aside from that she is a minor character in the New Testament.

As with so many women of the Bible, Mary Magdalene suffers from a rather troubled reputation. The damage done to her reputation and the others over the last two millennia is largely unfair. More than five hundred years after she lived, Pope Gregory the Great declared that the repentant, sinful woman who anointed Jesus' feet in Luke 7 was Mary Magdalene. Luke 7 does not identify the name of the woman, and it would be odd for it to be Mary Magdalene, since just a few verses later in Luke 8:2, we are introduced to her and told that Jesus cast seven demons out of her. Yet despite the improbability that Pope Gregory was correct in his assertion, the idea that Mary Magdalene was a woman of ill repute has maintained a constant foothold throughout church history.

In the modern age, one reason why Mary Magdalene is so popular seems to be precisely because so little is said about her. To those skeptical of the Christian faith, and cynical of the truth of the Bible, Mary Magdalene's story is a shining example that the church has something to hide. Through no fault of her own, Mary Magdalene has proven to be the conspiracy theorist's best friend. It has been suggested that she was Jesus' secret lover, or perhaps even His wife, and that she bore Him children. These ideas have existed (and been debunked) for a long time, but that has not stopped scholarly as well as popular books, like the runaway bestselling novel *The Da Vinci Code* (Dan Brown) from putting forth Mary Magdalene as someone significantly different from the picture the New Testament paints of her.

Despite the fact that everyone seems to have an angle when it comes to Mary Magdalene, her place as the first witness to the risen Messiah makes her infinitely interesting. What we must not miss about the life of Christ is just how sovereign God is. Every detail about the death, burial, and resurrection of Jesus Christ was superintended by God to fulfill prophecies and to bring about redemption for mankind in the exact way and time that God intended. This is why we should pay special attention to God's choice of Mary Magdalene as the first witness of His resurrection.

First, we see in God's choice of Mary Magdalene that God's plan of redemption is often surprising. It is easy to malign her, and everyone else who followed Jesus, for not realizing that He would rise from the dead just as He said He would. Writing around AD 400, John Chrysostom, the Archbishop of Constantinople, had this to say about Mary Magdalene:

> Full of feeling somehow is the female sex, and more inclined to pity. I say this, lest you should wonder how it could be that Mary wept bitterly at the tomb, while Peter was in no way so affected. For, "The disciples," it says, "went away unto their own home," but she stood shedding tears. Because hers was a feeble nature, and she as yet knew not accurately the account of the Resurrection.[2]

With such condescension, one has to consider the possibility that John Chrysostom's singleness was due to more than his vow of celibacy, but the truth is that his rather harsh treatment of Mary Magdalene isn't all that unusual, though most of us might not be so harsh, or let the men, such as Peter, off as easily. Two thousand years later, it is quite easy to forget that what Jesus did through His death and resurrection was nothing if not a complete surprise. NO ONE SAW THIS COMING! Even if it seems obvious now, it certainly wasn't then.

Second, we see in God's choice of Mary Magdalene that God's plan of redemption is often heartbreaking. Mary loved Christ deeply. Her devotion and passion for Jesus was evident, and the inhuman crucifixion of Jesus crushed her. She was oblivious to the fact that in three short days her anguish would turn to joy. When Jesus cast those demons out of her, He knew that her deliverance would result in great suffering.

Third, we see in God's choice of Mary Magdalene that God's plan of redemption is not based in any way on human reasoning. Appearing to Mary was not a move that garnered relevance and respectability for the infant Christian faith in the first century. According to the ancient historian Flavius Josephus, women were not eligible to serve as witnesses in a court of law.[3] Appearing first to Mary Magdalene did not scream "CREDIBILITY!" to the first recipients of the gospel message, but none of that mattered in God's plan. Human reasoning did not bring the gospel about, and human reasoning did not perpetuate it.

In His infinite wisdom, God chose Mary, from the little town of Magdala, to be the first witness to the resurrection of the Christ. It was a choice that made no earthly sense, but it was a choice that has had eternal repercussions for two thousand years.

By the Numbers

Number of times Mary Magdalene is mentioned in the Gospels: 12

Number of demons cast out of Mary Magdalene: 7

Things We Wondered

Luke 8:2–3 says that Mary Magdalene and the group of women who accompanied Jesus on His travels provided for

Jesus "out of their means." Where did Mary Magdalene come by her means?

Exactly who went where and when on Easter morning?

What happened to Mary Magdalene after the resurrection?

20

Mary and Martha

The Sisters

Mary, the sister of Lazarus, with great delight made one amongst them; she seated herself at the feet of Jesus, in the posture of an humble disciple; and we have a great deal of reason to believe that Martha, his other sister, would gladly have been with her there; but domestic cares pressed hard upon her, and "she was cumbered with much serving." . . . This good woman comes to our Lord with too impatient a complaint; insinuating some little reflection, not only on Mary, but on himself too. "Lord, dost thou not care that my sister hath left me to serve alone? Bid her, therefore, that she help me." . . . Alas, Martha! The concerns of the soul are of so much greater importance than those of the body, that I cannot blame your sister on this occasion: I rather recommend her to your imitation, and caution you, and all my other friends, to be much on your guard, that in the midst of your worldly cares, you do not lose sight of what much better deserves your attention.[1]

—George Whitefield

Scripture References

Matthew 26; Mark 14; Luke 10; John 11–12

Biography

We encounter the New Testament's most famous pair of sisters, Mary and Martha, three times in the Gospels. We know from these accounts that they lived in the village of Bethany just east of Jerusalem.

The first recorded encounter that these two women had with Jesus and His disciples occurred as Jesus was traveling from Jerusalem up to the region of Galilee in the final year of His ministry. Jesus was welcomed into the home that the sisters and their brother shared. Luke says specifically that the invitation was extended by Martha, so it is certainly feasible that Martha was the oldest, or at least the most assertive concerning matters of the daily operations of the home in Bethany.

Martha did exactly what we would expect. She went to work, busily preparing the meal for her distinguished and well-known guest. Mary, on the other hand, ignored the necessary preparations and sat at Jesus' feet, listening to His teaching. Martha approached Jesus, we might assume in a bit of a huff, and said, "Lord, do You not care that my sister has left me to do all the serving alone? Then tell her to help me" (Luke 10:40 NASB). At first, we might be tempted to lend Martha a sympathetic ear; certainly every older sister is reading this and nodding. But her statement chastised not only her sister, but ultimately Jesus for what He was allowing to take place. She has taken her sister to task for what amounts to laziness, and she has impugned Jesus for essentially being a willing co-belligerent to the stress that overwhelmed her at that moment. Christ's response stopped Martha. He responded to her chafing with a compassionate rebuke: "Martha, Martha, you are worried and bothered about so many things; but only one thing is necessary, for Mary has chosen the good part, which shall not be taken away from her" (Luke 10:41–42 NASB).

When next we encounter these sisters, a few months have passed, and Jesus is returning to Jerusalem from Galilee. When He arrives in Jerusalem, it will be one week before Passover, and His crucifixion. The sister's brother, Lazarus, was gravely ill, and they sent word to Jesus, asking Him to come to them speedily to heal him. The message reached Jesus in Jericho, but He did not travel to Bethany at once. John tells us that Jesus loved Mary, Martha, and Lazarus, but He delayed coming for two days. By the time Jesus leaves Jericho for Bethany, He knew that Lazarus was already dead. When He arrived, Lazarus had been in the tomb for four days.

When word reached the house that Jesus was approaching, Martha ran to meet Him while Mary stayed at the house. Martha met Jesus on His way, and their dialogue is some of the deepest theology in all of Scripture. Martha expresses disappointment and faith, saying to Jesus, "Lord, if You had been here, my brother would not have died. Even now I know that whatever You ask of God, God will give You." Jesus responded succinctly, telling her, "Your brother will rise again." Martha responded to Jesus with correct theology, saying, "I know that He will rise again in the resurrection on the last day." Now Jesus elaborates on His earlier statement, asking a probing question of Martha: "I am the resurrection and the life; he who believes in Me will live even if he dies, and everyone who lives and believes in Me will never die. Do you believe this?" She responded affirmatively, saying, "Yes, Lord; I have believed that You are the Christ, the Son of God, even He who comes into the world" (see John 11:21–27 NASB).

At the conclusion of her dialogue with Jesus, Martha leaves Him and returns to her home, where she pulls Mary aside and tells her secretly that Jesus is here and is asking for her. Mary quickly went to Jesus and met Him at the same place where He had been when He and Martha spoke. Mary fell at Jesus' feet and began to speak in much the same manner as her sister, saying, "Lord, if You had been here, my brother would not have died" (v. 32). Mary has all of Martha's grief, but we do not see the glimmer of hope exhibited by Martha. Jesus observes Mary's travail, and that of those around her, and He himself weeps out of compassion.

Jesus then inquired as to the location of Lazarus' tomb, which was a cave with a stone rolled in front of the entrance. Jesus commanded the stone to be rolled away from the tomb. To those in the area it must have seemed that Jesus, delirious from grief, wanted to see His friend's body one last time. Martha objected to moving the stone, reminding Jesus that by this time Lazarus' body would have begun to stink with decay after four days. Jesus reminded her of His words only moments earlier, saying, "Did I not say to you that if you believe, you will see the glory of God?" (v. 40). Then they removed the stone as He had commanded.

With the stone removed, Jesus prayed a prayer and then said three words that shook Mary and Martha to their core, "Lazarus, come forth" (v. 43). To the shock of Mary, Martha, everyone gathered, and we can only presume Lazarus himself, Lazarus came out of the tomb.

The third and final time that we come across these sisters is just a short time after the raising of Lazarus. The day is Saturday, the day before Palm Sunday, and less than a week before the crucifixion. Jesus is in Bethany at the home of Simon the Leper. A dinner was prepared, and in a move that should surprise no one, Martha is serving (although there are no outbursts).

At the meal, Mary approaches Jesus, carrying an alabaster jar full of about three-quarters of a pound of aromatic oil, which came from pure nard. She broke open the jar, poured it on His head, anointed His feet, and wiped His feet dry with her hair.

The fragrance of the perfumed oil wafted through the house, but not everyone in attendance was in awe of such a devoted and expensive display of worship. Only Judas objected to what Mary had done, viewing it as an extravagance and suggesting that the oil could have been sold and the money given to the poor. Of course, we know what those in the house (aside from Jesus) did not know: Judas wanted to help himself to a hefty cut before the poor would have received anything from the sale. Jesus responded, "Leave her alone. She did this in preparation for my burial. You will always have the poor among you, but you will not always have me" (John 12:7–8 NLT).

It is possible that during Passion Week Jesus actually commuted back and forth from Bethany to Jerusalem every day, staying in Bethany at night and teaching in Jerusalem during the day. Had He done this, it is likely that some of the time would have been spent in the company of these sisters. From this point on the biblical record is silent regarding Mary and Martha.

Role in Redemption

Consider the March sisters in *Little Women*, the Bennett sisters in *Pride and Prejudice*, and the Haynes sisters in *White Christmas*. There are some aspects about sisterhood that are universal: love, competition, jealousy, understanding, similarities, and differences. Each of these elements plays a part in the relationships of sisters the world over. Mary and Martha in the gospels of Luke and John are no exception.

The first of three encounters with Mary and Martha shows a bit of the competition and rivalry aspect of sisterhood. Jesus was traveling among the villages and stopped at the home of Martha and Mary. Mary, enthralled by the Lord and what He was teaching, sat at His feet to absorb His words. Martha, on the other hand, was caught up in the hustle and bustle of serving and hosting. She began to grow bitter and frustrated that her sister Mary was with the men, enjoying the presence of the Teacher, while she was slaving away with no help to serve an elaborate meal to their guests.

As I'm [Elaina] sitting here writing this chapter, it's my favorite time of year: Christmas. I revel in the decorations, activities, gifting, and general splendor that accompany this special celebration. But ironically, this also happens to be one of the most stressful times of the year for many, myself included. I have grand plans for crafting, baking, and merry-making that will make this season extra special and memorable for my children. But after reading of Martha's misplaced priorities, I can't help but think that my kids might prefer to have a mother who isn't quite so irritable rather than one who is absorbed with the many handprint crafts seen on Pinterest. Or that my husband would like to have a wife who isn't exhausted and stressed at the end of each day rather than an immaculate, beautifully decorated house. How much more would God rather I spend extra time in devotion to Him and celebrating the birth of His Son than running around from store to store to find that perfect gift?

This is what Jesus was saying to Martha when He said, "Martha, Martha, you are anxious and troubled about many things, but one thing is necessary. Mary has chosen the good portion, which will not be taken away from her" (Luke 10:41–42). Mary was not to be distracted by the trappings of a "good hostess." She was a sponge, soaking up every word her Lord said and showing her devotion to Him alone. But Martha, while hosting and serving guests, though not in itself a wrong action, allowed her priorities to be skewed, taking on so many extra duties rather than spending time at the feet of Jesus. Elaborate meals do not have an eternal impact on our lives, but sitting at the feet of Jesus will.

The second incident shows these two sisters, as different as they may be, united in grief over the loss of their beloved brother, Lazarus. Not only does this encounter the sisters had with Jesus give us some of the richest theology about our future resurrection and glorification in Christ, but it shows the deep and abiding love Jesus has for us.

Jesus purposely delayed going to help Lazarus when word of his sickness reached Him. He knew God would be more glorified through waiting a bit longer and bringing Lazarus back to life than by healing his illness immediately. When confronted by the grief of these two sisters, Jesus offers them hope: "I am the resurrection and the life. Whoever believes in me, though he die, yet shall he live, and everyone who lives and believes in me shall never die. Do you believe this?" (John 11:25–26).

Whereas Martha may have been rebuked by Jesus in the first story for her misplaced priorities, here she shows remarkable faith in the wake of tragedy. She boldly declares Jesus to be the Son of God who came to save the world. Not only did Martha find her own redemption in the person of Jesus, but she led her sister Mary to seek after the Messiah as well.

Martha went to Mary in private to let her know that Jesus had arrived and wanted to speak with her. Immediately, though she was grieving, Mary went to meet Him. This passage does not necessarily show Mary confessing faith in Jesus as her sister did, but it is evident that she did eventually in the next chapter. When Jesus saw how heartbroken Mary was over the death of her beloved brother, He showed His own grief. He must have known what would happen in the next few minutes—that He would call Lazarus out of the tomb and restore his life—but even so He exhibited vulnerability and showed His emotional anguish at the suffering of this family.

Jesus did call Lazarus out of the tomb, and many saw the miracle that occurred. Lazarus was allowed to die so that they could witness the power of Jesus' overcoming death and sustaining life. These sisters went through this tragedy so they could experience firsthand God's loving redemption.

The last event mainly involves Mary; Martha is barely mentioned. Six days before the Passover, Jesus was again visiting Bethany in the home of Lazarus. Martha was again serving their guests, and Mary had again joined the men to listen to Jesus speaking. This time, however, Mary acted boldly and anointed the feet of Jesus with some expensive ointment.

An extravagant gesture such as this naturally was met with criticism from some, mainly Judas, who thought she should have sold the ointment and given the money to the poor. But Jesus understood the significance. He responded to the criticism by saying, "Leave her alone, so that she may keep it for the day of my burial. For the poor you always have with you, but you do not always have me" (John 12:7–8). Even on this night, Jesus knew that He would soon sacrifice His life, and knew that Mary's act was an appropriate token of her devotion and humility before the Lord.

Despite their differences and their rough edges, Jesus used each of these two sisters to help accomplish His mission on earth. To Martha, Jesus declared His power to overcome death and sustain our life, and she in turn confidently pronounced faith in Him as the Messiah. Mary remained silent for most of her appearances in the Bible, but her actions shouted loudly of her devotion to the One who redeems us all.

By the Numbers

Miles to the east Bethany is from Jerusalem: 1.5

Miles from Jericho to Bethany: 12 to 15

Days Lazarus was in the grave before being resurrected by Jesus: 4

Approximate ounces of expensive oil used by Mary to anoint Jesus: 11

Number of years' wages represented by 300 denarii: 1

Things We Wondered

What was the birth order of Mary, Martha, and Lazarus?

From where did Mary get the pound of expensive ointment she used to anoint Jesus' feet?

Did Jesus spend nights with this family during Passion Week?

21

The Woman at the Well

The Town Crier

Jesus knew all about this woman. He knew that her life was bankrupt. She had not stopped trying to find happiness. Five times she had married, and every time she had entered into a marriage she had thought: "This is the one that will make me happy. This is the one that will last." However, none of her marriages had lasted, and now she was living with somebody who was not her husband. Why was she doing that? Was it because she wanted to be sinful? No. She simply wanted to find happiness. She was lonely and empty. She was willing to grab at anything that might satisfy her thirst.[1]

—R. C. Sproul

Scripture Reference

John 4

Biography

While Jesus was passing through Samaria on His way to Galilee, He stopped at a town called Sychar. It was in this town, at Jacob's well (Genesis 33:18–20), where Jesus encountered the woman at the well.

It was about noon, and being weary from His travels, Jesus sat down to rest beside the well. The fact that the gospel of John mentions that it was noon is significant because it was the hottest part of the day, and later than the typical time most women would have drawn water for the day.

But this particular Samaritan woman, whose name is not mentioned, went to the well by herself after the other women had already finished their chore. This woman probably avoided the company of other women because of her immoral lifestyle. We learn later, during the course of her conversation with Jesus, that she was living in sin with a man who was not her husband. This fact would have placed her on the outskirts of "acceptable" society, and would have created a natural barrier to relationships with other women in the town.

When Jesus saw the woman approach the well, he initiated a conversation with her by asking for a drink of water. Jesus was alone because the disciples traveling with Him had gone into the city to buy food. The woman was a bit skeptical at Jesus' request and questioned why a righteous Jewish man such as himself would ask anything of a Samaritan, much less a woman. In those days, Jews did not consider the Samaritans as part of God's chosen people. They were descendants of Jews who intermarried with Gentiles, and thus were viewed by the Jews as inferior. It would also have been rare for a man to speak with a woman in public, as it would have been considered by some as improper.

Jesus responds to the woman's skepticism by saying, "If you knew the gift of God, and who it is that is saying to you, 'Give me a drink,' you would have asked him, and he would have given you living water" (John 4:10). Understandably, the woman was confused and questioned how Jesus was going to get this living water since He had nothing with which to draw water. Perhaps she began to suspect there was something more than met the eye about this stranger, because she also asked Him if He was greater than their mutual forefather Jacob.

Jesus answered her question about His identity with what seems like a vague non-answer:

> "Everyone who drinks of this water will be thirsty again, but whoever drinks of the water that I will give him will never be thirsty again. The water that I will give him will become in him a spring of water welling up to eternal life."
>
> John 4:13–14

It might seem as if Jesus is merely continuing on with the conversation about water without addressing the woman's inquiry about His identity, but after peeling back the surface layer of His words we can see Him asserting His authority and power to give people eternal life. The woman, misunderstanding Jesus' true meaning of water that can take away a person's thirst for good, quickly jumped at the chance to never have to make the tiresome trek out to the well to draw water again. As a busy mom of three little blessings, I [Elaina] have to admit that the thought of never dealing with endless piles of laundry or dishes again would be enough to quickly take over my rational thoughts, preventing me from hearing anything else the person offering this life-changing gift might say.

It would have been highly unusual for a man to give a woman such a gift, so Jesus used the opportunity to see what the woman would tell Him about herself. It's obvious from His interaction with her that He already knew the answers to the questions

He asked, but the woman showed honesty and integrity when she answered truthfully that she had no husband. When Jesus confirmed that He knew her answer to be true, He also went further to say He knew she had had five husbands and the man she was living with currently was not her husband.

It's at this point in their conversation when you might envision a cartoon light bulb appearing over the woman's head. This man clearly knew intimate details about her life, though she had never met Him. Her best guess of His true identity was a huge understatement: "Sir, I perceive that you are a prophet" (John 4:19). Perhaps expecting judgment from Him, she deflected His comments about her personal life and instead observed that many Jews reviled the Samaritans for worshiping God on Mount Gerizim rather than at the temple in Jerusalem.

Jesus mirrored her deflective move, and rather than being drawn into a theological debate, stayed on target with His gospel message. The woman confessed having faith in a coming Messiah and must have been utterly astonished when Jesus confirmed that He was indeed the Messiah she was expecting.

It was at this point that the disciples returned to find Jesus deep in conversation with a strange woman. As the apostle John points out, they certainly must have been thinking to themselves, "What is Jesus doing?!" but none of them gave voice to their thoughts. Despite their restraint, the woman used this interruption as a good time to leave and tell the people in her town all that she had heard from Jesus. Either out of curiosity or incredulity, the townspeople followed her to meet this peculiar man. Jesus and the disciples stayed for two days among the people at Sychar before continuing on to Galilee.

This woman who lived outside the bounds of socially acceptable behavior, and who was probably shunned because of her sinful lifestyle, was the means by which many Samaritans from that town believed in Jesus as the Messiah. Her testimony sparked the curiosity of the townspeople and led them to seek out Jesus and hear of the Messiah's coming for them.

Role in Redemption

Jesus' conversation with the woman at the well in Samaria came at an interesting time for the disciples. More than likely this conversation took place in the first years of Jesus' public ministry. At this point, He had been publicly baptized by John the Baptist, chased money changers out of the temple with a whip, transformed water into wine at a wedding, and met with Nicodemus. John the Baptist had just been imprisoned for bringing Herod's wickedness to light, and now Jesus, with His disciples in tow, headed back to His home region of Galilee, traveling through the disdained Samaria.

A brief respite in Sychar to rest and gather sustenance led to an encounter between Jesus and someone highly unlikely to be viewed by His disciples as a possible convert. From this conversation there were two things readily apparent: This woman was missing something, even though it was doubtful she knew what it was; and what she needed in her life was staring her right in the face.

Divorce is far easier to come by and much less of a stigma in the twenty-first century than in the first. Yet even in today's permissive society, a person living with someone on the other side of five marriages would raise some eyebrows. It is clear from this woman's life before she met Jesus that she was incomplete in some way, and she knew it. The endless cycling through prospective mates shows a woman trying to fill a vacancy. More to the point, this woman's relationship history shows a woman with a thirst that she had been unable to quench with human relationships.

Jesus rightly pointed to this woman's real need, but she reacted like most of us do when the truth, even when it heals, hurts. Jesus' all too detailed recitation of her attempts to quench her thirst led her to propose a theological question to someone she underwhelmingly referred to as "a prophet." Knowing of the ethnic differences between Jesus and herself, and of the theological differences between Samaritans (who only believed the Pentateuch) and the Jews (who believed the entire Old Testament), she sought to divert the conversation to something that was a hot topic of that day, and, more important, did not involve her personally.

Jesus did not get sucked into her attempt at theological debate, but instead neatly cut to the heart of the issue. He responded,

> Woman, believe Me, an hour is coming when neither in this mountain nor in Jerusalem will you worship the Father. You worship what you do not know; we worship what we know, for salvation is from the Jews. But an hour is coming, and now is, when the true worshipers will worship the Father in spirit and truth; for such people the Father seeks to be His worshipers. God is spirit, and those who worship Him must worship in spirit and truth.
>
> John 4:21–24 NASB

As stated by Dr. Thomas Constable, "[Jesus] told the woman that the real issue was not *where* God's people had worshiped Him in the past, but *how* they would worship Him in the future."[2]

Few people were confronted personally by Jesus in this manner. Jesus is not teaching a group. It is just Him, a Jewish man, and this Samaritan woman. Conversation between these two would be awkward to begin with, but now one of them is revealing to the other that He is who she had been searching for her entire life.

Two thousand years later, the Samaritan woman serves as a giant beacon, proclaiming God's redemption. She was a woman who clearly evidenced a need for a Savior. Her whole life she had been crying out for something or someone who would make her whole. The fact that she had moved from marriage to being in a relationship without the marital commitment demonstrates that she was less and less hopeful she would ever find what she was looking for. One can assume that even she did not have much hope that the sixth time would be a charm.

One day she went to draw water and came face-to-face with the redemptive refreshment that her soul had always ached for. Decades of anticipation and desire came to fruition after she stopped at that well where the unknown Jewish man was resting. Many of her fellow citizens believed in Jesus, and their testimony to her was: "No longer do we believe because of your words, for we have heard for ourselves, and we know that this one really is the Savior of the world" (John 4:42 NET).

By the Numbers

Husbands of the Samaritan woman: 5

Time of day when Jesus' conversation with the Samaritan woman took place: 12:00

Days Jesus stayed in Sychar after His conversation with the woman by the well: 2

Miles from Jerusalem to Sychar: 30

Miles from Sychar to Capernaum, Jesus' likely destination in Galilee: 55

Things We Wondered

Did anybody ever get Jesus His drink of water?

What exactly was the woman's life like before she met Jesus?

Why did the woman get married and divorced so many times?

22

The Bleeding Woman

The Woman Healed by Her Faith

> The case seems hopeless, but hearing about Jesus gives her hope, and more than hope: faith so strong as to believe that merely touching his clothing will save her from her malady and, because of the crowd and her approaching him from behind, will save her without his even noticing either her or her touch. Such is Jesus' reputation for power.[1]
>
> —Robert H. Gundry

Scripture References

Matthew 9; Mark 5; Luke 8

Biography

Imagine that you live in ancient Galilee, a woman of marriageable and childbearing age. Yet instead of having your deepest desires fulfilled, instead of cuddling a sweet baby in your arms and enjoying attention from your husband, you are alone and utterly desperate. For years you have been afflicted with a disease that demands that you be isolated from any other human being, including your closest friends and family. The bleeding woman we encounter in the Gospels existed in these circumstances for over a decade: hopeless, forlorn, and forsaken.

Jesus was ministering in and around Galilee with His disciples, drawing crowds that followed Him wherever He went. One day, when He was speaking to the crowds, a synagogue leader named Jairus intercepted Jesus and begged that the Teacher save his critically ill daughter's life. Jesus rose to follow him but was still pressed in by the crowd on every side.

Suddenly, He stopped and turned to inquire of the crowd, "Who touched my garments?" (Mark 5:30). You can imagine the disciples' incredulity that Jesus wanted to know who had touched Him in the sea of people. Yet Jesus felt that single touch and knew what had transpired.

The person who touched Him was a woman, so desperate to be healed of her affliction that she risked even the forbidden to touch the hem of His garment. In this culture, and according to Jewish Law, bleeding was declared to be unclean. And not only was the person bleeding unclean, but any person or piece of furniture they touched was also unclean. Thus, this woman, who had suffered for twelve years, was in a perpetual state of uncleanness. Her life probably would have been no different than that of a leper, save that she was allowed to live within the city walls rather than be banished outside the gates.

Her decision to be among the crowd in the first place, much less to touch the garment of the spiritual leader, showed courage and desperation. The woman's faith was so great that she believed Jesus could heal her if only she touched the hem of His garment. She dared not risk further humiliation by approaching

Him and asking to be healed. And it was doubtful she could have gotten close enough to make her request known.

So knowing she was rendering every person around her unclean, she tried to hide her presence and the fact that she had succeeded in her mission by vanishing into the crowd. But Jesus felt the healing power leave His body and knew someone had touched Him. Indeed, the woman's bleeding stopped the second her hand grasped His garment, and she was completely cured.

Though she had received the healing she so desperately wanted, the woman did not escape before Jesus began searching for the person responsible. This woman showed tremendous courage and strength of character by returning and confessing her action. She may have been terrified and trembling, but she told Him the truth.

Rather than rebuking her or harshly judging her for disobeying the Law, Jesus showed compassion. He said, "Daughter, your faith has made you well; go in peace, and be healed of your disease" (Mark 5:34). Jesus recognized the magnitude of her faith and rewarded her for it.

Role in Redemption

Today, many struggle with the Bible's description of a menstruating woman as "unclean." Further investigation reveals that postpartum women were considered unclean for forty days as well. At times, the Old Testament laws regarding what today we view as normal bodily functions are used by skeptics to assail the Scriptures' alleged lack of respect for women.

The laws regarding uncleanness, however, were not exclusive to women. When the male reproductive system discharged outside of the act of sex, that man was also considered unclean with many of the same rules and regulations applied to a woman in the midst of a menstrual cycle. The laws that declared a woman to be impure during menstruation, and a man to be impure after a seminal discharge, point toward a larger principle that undergirded God's magnificent design for human reproduction.

The human reproductive system was designed to bring God glory through reproduction. This does not imply that the woman on her period, or the man who experienced a discharge, were sinful or viewed by God negatively in any way, but that those human reproductive processes designed by God for reproduction were, as we might say in the twenty-first century, temporarily off-line. As Old Testament scholar Joel M. Sprinkle summarized it,

> The reproductive processes which generate impurity in Levitical thought (Leviticus xii and xv) are all systemically dysfunctional; that is, they bar a male or female reproductive system from fulfilling its systemic purpose of reproducing human life. . . . A reproductive system which is incapable of reproducing life is not fully given over to (the creation of) life and, therefore, lacks "fullness of life." . . . Conversely, a reproductive system which is capable of reproducing life is fully given over to (the creation of) life and, therefore, possesses "fullness of life."[2]

Understanding the bigger picture of the Bible's treatment of both male and female uncleanness helps us to focus on two distinct ideas we see in the bleeding woman: intense suffering and desperate faith.

Many of the women in the Bible suffered greatly. Pain and sorrow were constant companions to the women whom God used. Yet even among these women, the woman who had a discharge of blood was conspicuous for what she endured. We do not know her name; in fact, we only know her by her infirmity. Though the Bible is rather light on medical specifics, even in the gospel by Dr. Luke, as best we can discern, this poor woman had been experiencing a menstrual discharge of blood for a period of twelve years. The physical, mental, and emotional distress caused by this torment had to have been excruciating.

Just how bad was this woman's trouble? We get a clear view of her quality of life by the use of the word *mastigoo* in Mark 5:29. Generally translated as disease or affliction in its most basic meaning, *mastigoo* also referred to "beating with a lash," "whipping," and "to scourge." This woman struggled for twelve years with a brutal disease, doctors who only made the problem worse, being considered unclean, and a condition that separated her from most social contact. A dozen years of torture had left this woman broken, bleeding, and feeling like she had been whipped day in and day out.

Because she was ceremonially unclean, she could not attend religious services. She could not bear children. If anyone shared a home with her, they could not touch her bed or any chair on which she sat without having to take a bath, wash their clothes, and be considered unclean until the evening. It is hard to gauge levels of suffering, and we must be careful not to compare who might have had things worse, but it is hard to argue with the idea that this woman's suffering exceeded that of any of the women we encounter in the Scriptures.

The reality of the bleeding woman's condition makes it far from a surprise that when Jesus, a man well-known for healing, came near, we find her exercising faith out of sheer desperation. Her condition was chronic, and no doubt it had demolished what life she had before this disease invaded her life. Attempts by physicians of her day to help had done the opposite. Treatments proved to be just as distressing as the proposed cures, ultimately made her ailment worse, and left her penniless in the process.

Jesus was a frequent visitor to the city of Capernaum, and we are left to wonder why a woman in such desperate need had not approached Him before. We will never know the answer to that question, but on this particular visit, most likely in Jesus' second year of public ministry, she was determined to see if this local carpenter turned teacher and healer was the answer to her problems. A crowd gathered and she made her move.

Of course, all of this had to be done in secret because she was unclean. Leviticus, chapter 15, prescribed seven days of uncleanness for a menstruating woman. Merely coming into contact with this woman meant that the person was unclean for the rest of the day. In a village whose population probably did not reach two thousand, she was putting everyone in the crowd, most of which probably knew her, and especially Jesus, at risk of being declared unclean. This explains why, even though the touch of Jesus' garment healed her, and she knew it immediately, she attempted to melt back into the crowd.

Jesus, however, would not allow her to simply disappear into the crowd. She was in great fear because of what she had done. The discovery of her action entailed everyone realizing the hazard in which she had put them. Her faith, desperate though it may have been, was appropriately placed. As one commentator stated, "She's healed for good. The Greek verbal form behind 'healed' indicates permanence. Jesus' power has eliminated any possibility of a relapse."[3] Few knew the debility of her suffering, but because of her boldness everyone knew the power of her faith.

By the Numbers

Number of years the woman with the issue of blood suffered: 12

Number of days the afflicted woman would have had to go without a flow of blood to be clean: 12

Days anyone who came into contact with a bleeding woman would be unclean: 1

Things We Wondered

Where did the woman get the money to pay for physicians?

Were Jesus and the other people in the crowd obligated to complete the cleansing rituals because the woman had touched them?

23

The Syrophoenician Woman

The Believing Beggar

> The woman by her persistent plea demonstrated her faith in the person of Christ. She, a Gentile (dog), asked for what the children (Israel) cast aside. Because of that faith her request was granted; her daughter was healed immediately.[1]
>
> —J. Dwight Pentecost

Scripture References

Matthew 15; Mark 7

Biography

Jesus had been ministering in Palestine for a while, and the amount of resistance and rejection He experienced from the Jews began to increase. He left Galilee and headed to the primarily

Gentile region of Tyre and Sidon. Here, He hoped to fly under the radar for a bit, but escape from the constant crowds was impossible. Word of His presence at a house became known to a woman identified to us only as the Syrophoenician woman.

This woman was a Gentile, and she was desperate to find Jesus so He could help her daughter. She had heard of Jesus' reputation for healing others and knew He would be able to free her daughter from the demon that possessed her. So when the woman finally reached Jesus, she threw herself at His feet and begged for His help.

Up to this point, Jesus had shown extraordinary compassion for those who came to Him for help. But with this woman, Jesus' initial response was silence. When He does finally speak to her, His answer seems almost callous: "I was sent only to the lost sheep of the house of Israel. . . . It is not right to take the children's bread and throw it to the dogs" (Matthew 15:24–26).

Though His words must have felt like a dagger in her heart, the woman persisted. She knew that as a Gentile she was not part of God's chosen people of Israel, and her reply showed both humility and great faith. The woman said, "Yes, Lord, yet even the dogs eat the crumbs that fall from their masters' table" (Matthew 15:27).

Jesus was amazed at the woman's response and immediately rewarded her great faith. He sent her on her way home with assurances that her daughter was liberated from the unclean spirit. Not needing a second invitation, the woman went straight home and found that Jesus' words were true. Her daughter was healed and was lying in bed with no sign of the demon that had previously possessed her.

Role in Redemption

The Syrophoenician woman is not one of the more popular women in the Bible. There aren't a lot of sermons about her, and she is not the subject of any bestselling book. No songs have been written about her. We don't even know her name so we have to refer to her by her ethnicity. Her interaction with Jesus is awkward at best, and yet she is one of the most remarkable women you will make the acquaintance of in all of God's Word.

The infrequency with which the Syrophoenician woman is discussed is a shame because she gives us such a unique perspective on Jesus. We love the Jesus who raises Lazarus from the dead, walks on water, heals the lame, and makes the blind to see. We are inspired by His parables, His compassion for those in need, and His willingness to call the religious leaders of the day hypocrites. The Jesus we meet via the Syrophoenician woman is, at first glance, almost a different version from the One we see elsewhere in the Gospels. He comes across in both Matthew and Mark as rude and rather short in His interaction with a mother pleading on behalf of her daughter. This is not the Jesus we expect.

Jesus had for some time been ministering in and around His home region of Galilee. The gospels of Matthew and Mark both record a short excursion He makes from Galilee to the predominantly Gentile area of Tyre and Sidon. His conversation with this woman is the only recorded event from this trip.

When word reached this woman that Jesus was in the area, she determined to do whatever was necessary to see Jesus act on behalf of her daughter, who was demon possessed. Matthew's account gives us the additional detail that this demon possession was severe. English translations use terms like *severely, miserably, cruelly,* or *grievously* to translate the Greek word *kakōs*. This word is defined by one Greek dictionary as signifying "a high point on a scale of extent and implying harm and seriousness." If there was a scale for demon possession and ten was the highest, this little girl's experience was a ten. This woman's daughter was not simply possessed—demon possessions were never good or pleasant experiences—but on that scale she was suffering tremendously.

Of course this woman would seek out Jesus, doing anything to get an audience with the One she had heard could cast out demons, but Jesus does not initially respond. Then, as we likely would, she increased the volume, agitating the less-than-compassionate disciples in the process, and then she threw herself in Jesus' path, making sure He had to interact with her. When Jesus does respond, He tells her that it is not her turn to be helped, and He does so with an illustration that essentially puts this woman and her daughter in the place of a dog.

Critics read this story and condemn Jesus for His response. He is often accused of bigotry or callousness. These reactions to the story are off-base for a couple of reasons. First, remember where this conversation took place—not in Israel. These comments by Jesus were not spoken while surrounded by Jews, but largely by Gentiles. Second, the woman's reaction and Jesus' response tell us about both of their motives.

The woman is completely undeterred by Jesus' initial refusal to hear her request. Rather than taking offense, she seems to take the perspective that this is merely another obstacle to overcome. She is fighting for her daughter's life and has no intention of being stopped, because she believes that His intervention is the answer to her problem. She may have been slightly offended, but the importance of her request made her persist. She had a big problem and she needed a big solution.

Jesus' answer shows us that His method of interaction with this woman, which was almost adversarial, was also intentional. Jesus wanted to see this woman's faith. Did she possess a determined faith in Him or was she merely taking a shot in the dark? If the demon possession ranked a ten, how high did her faith rank? The answer is that when Jesus healed her daughter, even from a distance, He told her that her faith was great.

One of the toughest experiences of faith is wanting to follow God but feeling like the biggest obstacle is God himself. Does God want to help us? Is He truly good? This woman was not the only person Jesus treated this way. When the rich young ruler approached Jesus a few chapters later in Mark, He initially rebuffed him, saying, "Why do you call Me good?" What Jesus did often in the Gospels was to ask a question that revealed someone's heart. The rich young ruler showed that he lacked faith, but this Gentile woman evidenced that she had faith and she would not be deterred even when Jesus seemed ambivalent to her overwhelming problem.

The Syrophoenician woman's faith resulted in her daughter getting her life back from the clutches of evil. This mother's experience was not easy. Yet she shows us that God's method of redemption in our lives is not always simple and is rarely the same. God worked a mighty act of redemption in her life primarily because she refused to back down.

By the Numbers

Miles from Capernaum to Tyre: 35

Miles from Capernaum to Sidon: 50

Things We Wondered

How old was the Syrophoenician woman's daughter?

How did the demon manifest itself in her life?

24

Widow with Two Mites

The Woman Who Gave All

SHE went her way, and never knew
The praise which from her Savior's lips she drew;
Yet casting all
Before the Temple door,
We must believe
She never wanted more.[1]

—Marjory Clifford

Scripture References

Mark 12; Luke 21

Biography

While Jesus and His disciples were in Jerusalem at the temple, they took seats in the treasury courtyard, where they could watch people putting money into the offering box. They would have seen a variety of people at the temple, from the very rich to the very poor.

The Bible says that they did, in fact, see many rich people put in large sums of money. Because these people were very wealthy, their offerings were probably not so much sacrificial as obligatory. They gave because that's what people did in the temple.

However, Jesus quickly drew the disciples' attention to see a poor widow drop two small copper coins into the treasury. These coins added together equaled about the worth of one penny in today's American currency. He said to them,

> Truly, I say to you, this poor widow has put in more than all those who are contributing to the offering box. For they all contributed out of their abundance, but she out of her poverty has put in everything she had, all she had to live on.
>
> Mark 12:43–44

Role in Redemption

The unnamed widow who gave her only two mites tends to receive more attention than the few verses dedicated to her would usually warrant. Her story of sacrificial giving has been used as motivation and inspiration, but there is a larger context to her story that is often missed. This widow was certainly an example of true giving, and what sacrifice looks like, but she also served a much greater purpose.

In Jesus' praise of this "poor widow," the words He used stand in stark contrast to His assessment of the scribes occurring in the preceding verses. Jesus had been holding court at the temple as the religious leaders of the nation of Israel sought to trap Him in controversy. They were pursuing Him surreptitiously because He was so popular among the people they were afraid to come and take Him by force. He responded to these attempts to snare Him, and then said in His teaching,

> "Beware of the scribes, who like to walk around in long robes, and love respectful greetings in the market places, and chief seats in the synagogues and places of honor at banquets, who devour widows' houses, and for appearance's sake offer long prayers. These will receive greater condemnation."
>
> Luke 20:46–47 NASB

In the first century, even the lowest paid laborer would have earned two mites in just a matter of minutes on the job. The travesty of what Jesus and His disciples were observing was that the widow's gift was so small as to be almost unnoticeable. Yet the scribes strutted around the temple complex and the rest of Jerusalem like preening peacocks while their actions left widows, such as this one, devoid of the basic necessities.

Temporally speaking, this woman's gift was wasted. It was impossibly small, and no doubt the corrupt religious officials ensured that gifts were used improperly. The very people who were supposed to ensure that widows were taken care of were the people who were abusing and devouring widows in pursuit of their own desires.

Eternally speaking, this woman's gift has been earning dividends for nearly two thousand years. The motivation to give sacrificially in obedience to God meant that this woman had done more with her two small coins than the most elaborate of gifts. She was a poor widow, but Jesus held her up as a standard that the wealthy and the powerful could not attain.

The Scriptures promise that one day God will give to each person the rewards they have earned by their faith and obedience to Him. Many famous Christians will receive their rewards, and we will all be impressed. Then God will turn His attention to a little old lady none of us have ever heard of, and heaven's vault will open up to display her many great rewards. This widow's gift did more to further the kingdom of God than we may ever know.

By the Numbers

Mites placed by the widow in the temple collection: 2

Minutes of labor it took to make two mites: 5

Things We Wondered

Why were Jesus and the disciples watching the people put money in the offering boxes in the first place?

How did Jesus know the two copper coins were everything this widow had with which to live?

25

The Widow of Nain

The Recipient of Compassion

In the story of the resuscitation of the widow's son, we see the powerful reversal of death. Jesus deals here with the most fundamental obstacle we will ever face. If death were the end, then there would be no hope in this life or after (1 Corinthians 15:12–19). The judgment of God would make no sense, nor would his claim to restore and redeem us. Thus this miracle testifies to a central aspect of Christian hope. Its touching image reminds us that renewal and reunion are not an impossible dream. God promises to restore to life those who know his touch. In Jesus, God takes the initiative to accomplish this renewal.[1]

—Darrell Bock

Scripture Reference

Luke 7

Biography

Jesus was traveling around Galilee when He and His disciples, followed by a great crowd, came to a town called Nain. It is located southwest of the Sea of Galilee, near Mount Tabor. As they were approaching the town gate, Jesus and His followers encountered a funeral procession. According to the customs of the time, the widow would have led the procession and any people in the town would have stopped whatever they were doing to join the procession when it passed by.[2]

A man, the only son of a widow, had died and was being carried out for burial. This would have been devastating for the widowed mother, as she probably had no way of providing for herself after the loss of her husband and son. She most likely was staring down the road to a long and desperate life of poverty.

When Jesus saw this grieving woman, He had compassion on her and said, "Do not weep" (Luke 7:13). In the midst of grief and hopelessness, His words must have felt like salt rubbing on an open wound. At the very least, they probably sounded ridiculous to the woman.

Jesus then approached the funeral bier and touched the body of the dead man. According to the strict Law of the Jews, touching a dead body made one unclean and required purification before that person could be clean again. Nevertheless, Jesus touched the young man's body and said, "Young man, I say to you, arise" (Luke 7:14). Immediately, the dead man received life again and sat up and began to talk.

The crowd, astonished by the miracle they had just witnessed, were gripped by fear and began to glorify God. They recognized that Jesus was God's Son and immediately began spreading the news of everything they had seen and heard throughout Judea.

Role in Redemption

In some ways, the story of the widow of Nain is light on details. Like many of the women in the Bible, we do not know her name. We do not know how long she had been widowed, and we do not know the age of the son she was mourning. However, there are two details we do know from the story, and they present to us a striking picture. First, we know the perilousness of this widow's situation. Second, we know the mighty power God evidenced in her life.

It may seem harsh to put it this way in the twenty-first century, but in the world of the first century, this woman's life was essentially over. She was dependent on her husband, and later her son, for protection and provision. With both of them gone, she would have to depend on other, more distant relatives, or perhaps even public charity. In that culture, communities tended to be much more connected than they are now, but her situation would certainly be hazardous. Consider this summary by one scholar:

> For the post-menopausal woman, with no remaining reproductive potential (and perhaps limited remaining potential for hard physical labor), the situation of childlessness presented a greater threat to survival. . . . Even if a widow had sufficient resources to live on, her detachment from a male-headed family meant she had no representation in judicial matters, and she might easily be defrauded of what was rightfully hers. If the loss of her husband did not leave her destitute, her lack of anyone to represent her in the justice system made the slide into abject poverty all too easy. These are the widows of the biblical ethical injunctions—women without husband or household, and without hope of securing either. . . . With no remaining value to the society and no one on earth to protect her, she epitomizes the powerless and vulnerable one whose only hope is in the ethical demands of Yahweh.[3]

We do not know this widow's financial situation, but it is clear that her future was at best bleak. The death of her son would have obliterated the foundational things she counted on. Her connection to her husband's family, with whom she probably lived, would be severed. She had no earning potential, and what is worse, she would be easy prey for those who sought to take advantage of her legally. This is the scene that Jesus, His disciples, and the large crowd happened upon as they entered the tiny village of Nain.

Though it is still reasonably early in Jesus' ministry, the large crowd that followed Him into Nain had grown to expect the miraculous, but even they were certainly surprised at what transpired. At this point in His ministry, Jesus had not raised anyone from the dead. It had been hundreds of years since the power of God was exhibited in such a way. No doubt the crowd knew the stories of the people raised from the dead by Elijah and Elisha, but those stories were practically ancient history by this time.

Jesus' actions in this circumstance were very specific. Interrupting a funeral procession was incomprehensible to the manners and customs of the first century. His touching of an open coffin, which carried a dead man, meant that He would be unclean for at least a day (Numbers 19:21–22), and if He touched the dead body itself He would be unclean for an entire week (Numbers 5:2–3; 19:11–20). Jesus openly breached protocols that had been in place for centuries, and His rationale was compassion for this devastated widow.

Funerals took place quickly after death in those days because of decomposition and no method of preserving the body. The tragedy that had befallen this woman was still fresh. No doubt she had little time to begin to come to terms with the precipice over which her life had just stumbled. None of that mattered to Jesus. The cleanliness laws that were put in place existed to prevent disease from spreading, but Jesus had the power of life.

This widow's life was a total wreck, but her tragedy was turned into rejoicing. The people responded to God's reversal of this woman's calamity by saying, "God has visited His people!" No doubt the widow of Nain would agree.

By the Numbers

Sons of the widow of Nain: 1

Days someone who touched a dead person was considered unclean: 7

This was the first individual resurrection of the New Testament, and the first performed by Jesus. Number of resurrections performed in the Bible: 9

Things We Wondered

How old was this widow? And how old was her son who died?

What happened to this woman's husband? How long had she been a widow?

How did the mourners react when Jesus interrupted the funeral procession?

Having seen Jesus perform other miracles, were the disciples as afraid as the rest of the crowd?

26

The Woman Sinner

The Woman Forgiven of Much

> The woman in Luke's anointing is described at the outset as "a sinner." Yet Luke writes the narrative in such a way that the reader discovers that "sinner" is no longer an adequate way to describe her. The woman is to be seen as released from her sins and thereby as a whole and fully restored member of the community.[1]
>
> —Jennifer A. English

Scripture Reference

Luke 7

Biography

In the second year of Jesus' ministry, He was traveling in the region of Galilee accompanied by the disciples. While Jesus was in Galilee with His disciples, a Pharisee named Simon requested that He and the others attend a banquet at his house. During the course of the meal, a woman, with a well-known reputation as a sinner, approached Jesus at His place at the table. Many have speculated that her sins were sexual, such as prostitution, but the Scriptures do not give us details as to her sins.

The woman's appearance at a formal meal was not necessarily unusual, as social customs of the time made allowances for needy people to visit such homes in order to partake of the meal's leftovers. Though her appearance at the banquet was not out of place, her position certainly was. According to one scholar, "In banquets where uninvited people could enter, they were to remain quiet and away from the couches, observing the discussions of host and guests."[2]

This woman, rather than remaining quiet and out of the way, approached the guest of honor, carrying a vial of perfume made of alabaster. Because of the nature of meals being served in the first century, it would make sense that she would come near the feet of Jesus. One commentator sums it up this way: "The sandals were removed at meals, and people reclined with their feet behind them; she could therefore easily approach the feet."[3] She came near Jesus and stood behind Him at His feet, which she began to wet with her tears. She bent down, wiping His feet with her hair and kissing them. Finally, she anointed them with the perfume from the alabaster box.

At the sight of this public spectacle, Simon the Pharisee thought to himself, *"If this man were a prophet, he would know what kind of woman is touching him. She's a sinner!"* (Luke 7:39 NLT). Imagine Simon's shock when he discovered that Jesus knew not only the type of woman who was touching Him but Simon's thoughts as well.

Jesus turned His attention to Simon and told him a story. The story was about a moneylender who had two debtors: one owed five hundred denarii, and the other fifty. The difference between these debts would be roughly that of two months' salary versus twenty months' salary for the average earnings of the time.[4] Despite the differences in debt amounts, both debtors were ultimately unable to pay, and the moneylender forgave them both. Jesus then asked Simon which debtor would love the moneylender more. Simon answered Him, saying, "I suppose the one who had the bigger debt forgiven" (Luke 7:43 NIV).

Jesus affirmed that Simon answered correctly. He then turned to the woman but continued to speak to Simon. Jesus offered a stern rebuke to the Pharisee:

> "Do you see this woman? I entered your house; you gave Me no water for My feet, but she has wet My feet with her tears and wiped them with her hair. You gave Me no kiss; but she, since the time I came in, has not ceased to kiss My feet. You did not anoint My head with oil, but she anointed My feet with perfume. For this reason I say to you, her sins, which are many, have been forgiven, for she loved much; but he who is forgiven little, loves little."
>
> Luke 7:44–47 NASB

As if this all had not been enough, Jesus now spoke to the woman and told her that her sins had been forgiven. The rest of the guests in attendance began to murmur among themselves, wondering exactly who Jesus was that He could forgive sins. Having forgiven her sins, Jesus sent the woman on her way, telling her, "Your faith has saved you; go in peace" (Luke 7:50).

At times, this incident with the woman sinner has been confused with an interaction that Jesus had with Mary, the sister of Martha and Lazarus. The two episodes share a lot of commonality: both women washed Jesus' feet using their tears and hair, and both carried alabaster boxes. There are, however, some significant differences that tip us off that these are two similar, but distinct, occurrences. The story of the woman sinner occurred in Jesus' second year of ministry in the region of Galilee. The story involving Mary took place just before Jesus' triumphal entry into Jerusalem in the town of Bethany, in the region of Judea. They are not the same incident, and it may even have been that Mary was inspired to mimic the woman's act of devotion.

Role in Redemption

It is a common propensity in our culture to compare ourselves to those around us. We are constantly taking measure of our physical looks, accomplishments, bank accounts, and social status, and then evaluating where we stand among our peers. This is exactly what Simon the Pharisee did when he noticed the attention the sinful woman lavished on Jesus. He scorned her because everyone knew her to be a sinner and congratulated himself on being more righteous than she. It also gave him an opportunity to look down on the apparent ignorance of Jesus, the untrained celebrity rabbi, who had the common rabble hanging around Him.

Little did Simon know that man's wisdom is counted as foolishness in the sight of God. He took it for granted that he, a Pharisee and law-abiding man, would be favored by God for his piety. Simon was oblivious to his need for redemption and felt that the brazen woman fawning over Jesus did not deserve deliverance at all. And to top it off, he felt that Jesus' lack of discernment over this woman's character diminished His status as a prophet to a mere teacher.

By contrast, the sinful woman saw clearly her own transgressions and the shame they brought. She knew she was a sinner in need of the Lord's salvation, and she was so overcome with love and gratitude for Jesus that she could do nothing less than humble herself at His feet. Her devotion to Jesus went above and beyond the accepted norm of hospitality. She anointed His feet not with scented olive oil, as was typical, but with an expensive alabaster flask of ointment. And even more than that, she wiped His feet with her hair and kissed them as a gesture of love. The sinful woman knew she desperately needed the redemption that only God could provide.

Jesus looked at the woman and saw past her poor decisions and her life of sin. Instead, He saw a woman who treasured the redemption He offered, and so Jesus unreservedly forgave her. His words of forgiveness caused quite a stir among the other banquet attendees. Only God had the right and the power to forgive sins. Who was this man claiming to have that same power? Was He, in fact, God?

The last words Jesus spoke to the sinful woman were the sweetest words she'd ever heard: "Your faith has saved you; go in peace" (Luke 7:50). No longer did she need to carry around her burden of guilt. She could put aside her anxiety and worry. She had been redeemed.

By the Numbers

Debtors in the parable told by Jesus: 2

Denarii owed by the first debtor: 500

Denarii owned by the second debtor: 50

Things We Wondered

Who exactly was this woman?

What were this woman's known sins?

Did Mary, the sister of Martha and Lazarus, intentionally mimic this woman's act of devotion?

27

Tabitha

The Resurrected Woman

The wake was under way, and the room where Dorcas had been laid was filled with friends, mostly widows, who stood weeping as they passed around afghans, sweaters and shawls—all crocheted by Dorcas. Everyone there had a story about how her life had touched theirs, some selfless act of devotion that she had performed for them. Dorcas, whose name means "gazelle," was a tireless disciple whose devotion to others inspired a network of support that undergirded an entire church community.[1]

—Jon M. Walton

Scripture Reference

Acts 9

Biography

During the time of the apostles, there was a woman named Tabitha who lived in Joppa. She was well-known for her faithful ministry and described in the Bible as "full of good works and acts of charity" (Acts 9:36). Though she was known for her kindness and charity, she is best known to us for being raised from the dead by the apostle Peter.

As a bit of background information, Tabitha's name translated into Greek is *Dorcas*. She lived in Joppa, which was the main seaport of Israel and is known today as Tel Aviv.

When Tabitha died, her loved ones washed and prepared her body and laid her in an upper room. Customarily, they would have buried her body as soon as possible, but the fact that they laid her body in an upper room while they searched for the apostle Peter indicates that they hoped for a miracle.

Joppa was near Lydda, the city where Peter was staying, and so the disciples of Joppa sent an urgent message for him to come immediately. Peter hurried to Joppa with them and found Tabitha's body in the upper room, surrounded by grieving widows. These widows knew Tabitha well, and were even wearing the tunics and other garments that Tabitha had made for them while she was alive.

Peter asked everyone to wait outside, and when he was alone he knelt beside her and prayed. According to one scholar, "Peter's procedure here was almost identical to that of Jesus when He raised Jairus's daughter. (Mark 5:41; Luke 8:51–56). Peter's praying shows that he was relying on Jesus for his power."[2]

As soon as Peter said, "Tabitha, arise," she opened her eyes and sat up. He presented her alive to the saints and the widows gathered outside the upper room, and the news of her miraculous resurrection spread throughout Joppa. Because of Tabitha's miracle, many believed in the Lord.

Role in Redemption

One of the difficulties in reading and applying the Bible is that, for all of the information we have, we really only know snippets about the people in the New Testament and how they put their theology into practice. We know precious little about Peter and Paul aside from a few incidents in each of their lives. Even our understanding of the life of Christ is based on a small sample of His life on earth. With such small snapshots, it can be difficult at times to discern themes or patterns in the life of a follower of Christ. What were their habits? We know that they proclaimed the gospel, but how did they interact with their fellow citizens? What things did they do to make a difference in the world around them in the name of Christ? Tabitha is an exception to this rule.

The life of Tabitha manages to give us a tremendous peek into her life and influence in just a few short verses. We see very little about her, but what we do see is powerful and telling. Primarily, there are two things about Tabitha that we see: what she did and how she did it. What she did includes two things: kindness and charity. We see just a bit later that a large portion of her kindness and charity was wrapped up in caring for the widows of Joppa. Specifically, she handmade tunics and other garments for these widows who were needy. *How* she did these things is just as important. The various Bible translations handle Acts 9:36 differently, but they all attempt to convey something that the Greek of the book of Acts is very clear on. Tabitha did not show kindness and charity just once. It was something she did repeatedly, out of habit. It was her custom, her demeanor, her way of life. English translations use terms like *always* and *continually* to bring out this facet of Tabitha's life.

When Tabitha encountered redemption, it did not leave her unchanged. She was a disciple of Christ who tirelessly worked to care for others. It is little wonder then that her death was a blow to the citizens of Joppa. Tabitha took the love and compassion of Christ and manifested it for those around her, particularly for those who were disadvantaged. The real impact of Tabitha's life was not in the fact that she was raised from the dead, but in how she lived before she died.

By the Numbers

People raised from the dead by Peter: 1

Approximate miles from Lydda to Joppa: 9

Things We Wondered

What was the cause of Tabitha's death?

What are the details of Tabitha's personal life? Was she married? Did she have children?

28

Phoebe

The Generous Servant

Phoebe was carrying the letter to the Romans, and letters sometimes identified special bearers. Phoebe's status is important, because as the letter's bearer who knew Paul's intention directly, she might read it (hence, "perform" it orally, and by gestures communicate his emphases and ironies) in the congregations in Rome; certainly she would be called on to explain elements if questions arose. They should welcome her, reciprocating her own hospitality to others (see Romans 16:1–2).[1]

—Craig S. Keener

Scripture Reference

Romans 16

Biography

Only two verses in the whole Bible mark the memory of Phoebe. She obviously lived a life that was both glorifying to God and valuable to her fellow believers. Paul marked her place in history in his letter to the Romans, and with two simple verses left an indelible impression on our minds.

Phoebe lived in Cenchreae, the seaport of Corinth. She is described as being a servant of the church there, which might entail the duties of a deaconess. Whether she formally held the office of a deaconess or not is not important. As Dr. Thomas Constable puts it, "It is unclear whether Phoebe held office as a deaconess or whether she was simply an informal servant of the church. Paul stressed her service, not her office."[2]

After this short introduction, Paul asked the believers in Rome to welcome Phoebe in the Lord. As part of their welcome, Paul expected that they would help her with whatever she may need. Paul was asking them to help Phoebe in the way she had helped those around her. Indeed, Paul said she was a patron, or helper, of many, including himself.

Phoebe's mention in the Bible may be small, but it is obvious that the effects of her service and faithfulness were far-reaching.

Role in Redemption

The city of Corinth was an isthmus, a narrow piece of land with water on two sides that formed a link between mainland Greece and the part known as the Peloponnese peninsula. Because this isthmus was so small, only four miles, it was often quicker for lighter ships to actually be hauled from one side of the isthmus to the other. This meant that Corinth had a port on one side named Lechaion and on the other named Cenchreae. These two ports were connected by a road called the Diolkos, on which ships were hauled from one port to the other and placed back in the water to continue their journey.

We know from the book of Romans that Cenchreae, the port on the eastern side of the Corinthian Isthmus, was the home of Phoebe. The book of Romans was written by the apostle Paul from the city of Corinth, probably in the winter of AD 56–57. Most commentators on the book of Romans believe that after Paul finished his letter to the church in Rome, it was carried there personally by Phoebe.

There are two much-debated words that the apostle Paul uses to describe Phoebe. The first is *servant*, a translation of the Greek term *diákonos*. This could refer to the official position of a deacon, or it could refer to someone who does other notable service on behalf of the church. The second is the word *patron*, or possibly *benefactor* or *helper*, depending on which English Bible you use, and it is a translation of the Greek term *prostatis*. Was Phoebe someone who simply helped the apostle, or was she in fact a benefactor for both he and the Corinthian church, supporting the ministry with her own financial resources?

Was she simply a member of the church in Cenchreae or something more official, such as a deaconess? The answer would help us a great deal as we look to the Scriptures to guide us regarding the role of women in the local church. What was implied by the words *servant* and *patron*? The answers to the questions about these two terms used of Phoebe are important, but if we are not careful we can get so bogged down in the hazy details of *what* Phoebe was that we miss the brilliantly clear picture of *who* she was.

Think about it this way: The book of Romans is frequently regarded as the bedrock of New Testament theology. Think of an analogy for something that is the most important, or the best, and there is an excellent chance that analogy has been used for the book of Romans. Unlike any other book in the entire

Bible, Romans proclaims the gospel, the work of Jesus Christ, and the basics of Christianity in ways that are easy to grasp while at the same time are incredibly complicated.

It was the study of the book of Romans that brought Martin Luther to an understanding that salvation was by faith alone. It would not be a stretch to say that the book of Romans was largely responsible for the Protestant Reformation. For his part, Luther always treasured the book of Romans, both for its role in his life and for its seminal place in New Testament theology. In his commentary on Romans, Luther had this to say:

> This letter is truly the most important piece in the New Testament. It is purest Gospel. It is well worth a Christian's while not only to memorize it word for word but also to occupy himself with it daily, as though it were the daily bread of the soul. It is impossible to read or to meditate on this letter too much or too well. The more one deals with it, the more precious it becomes and the better it tastes . . . it is in itself a bright light, almost bright enough to illumine the entire Scripture.[3]

It is this book, the bright shining star of all that God revealed to us in the Scriptures, which Paul entrusted to Phoebe. Ponder that for a moment. When the most important book in the entire Bible had to get from Corinth to Rome, God in His sovereignty saw to it that the right person for the job was His servant Phoebe. Often when we consider the letters of the New Testament, we think about the author, but we rarely stop to consider the carrier. We neglect this to our detriment. When Paul handed this letter to Phoebe, he was putting God's inspired words into her hands. He trusted her to do what was necessary to make the long, treacherous journey, hundreds of miles to Rome. When the conversation about Phoebe revolves around whether or not she was a servant in an official or an unofficial capacity, that debate neglects the fact that Phoebe was far more than a servant to Cenchreae in some capacity. Phoebe's trustworthiness and the service she rendered exceeded anything that she or the apostle Paul could have imagined. Without Phoebe, Martin Luther would have remained a Catholic monk in anguish over his sin and his inability to justify himself through good works. Without Phoebe, the Protestant Reformation as we know it never would have happened. Without Phoebe, the mountain peak of New Testament theology would have been obscured from our view.

Where would we be without Phoebe? The answer to that question is hard to determine. What we do know because of Phoebe is that we are sinners falling short of the glory of God, but are now justified by faith and have peace with God.

By the Numbers

Miles from Corinth to Rome: 617

Miles from Cenchreae to Corinth: 6.5

Things We Wondered

Why was Phoebe traveling from Cenchreae to Rome?

Did Phoebe financially support Paul's ministry and the church in Corinth?

Was her role as a servant of the Corinthian church formal or informal?

29

Lois and Eunice

The Women of Sincere Faith

When you look at your own family and you say "there are so many things messed up," just remember the power of God's promises in the lives of Eunice and Lois and Timothy. God sends His word forth, and it will not return without accomplishing what He has appointed it to accomplish. The power of the covenant of grace in the life of Timothy is manifested in the fruit borne by these two believing women. Mothers, don't ever underestimate what you are implanting in the lives of the children that God has given to you. Many a woman has been God's instrument to win her children to Christ . . . and her husband to Christ. May God grant that you follow in the line of Lois and Eunice.[1]

—J. Ligon Duncan III

Scripture References

Acts 16; 2 Timothy 1; 3

Biography

Lois and Eunice are two women we learn about in a roundabout way from the apostle Paul. We begin to learn of them as part of Timothy's family background in Acts 16.

Paul traveled to Lystra, where he met a disciple named Timothy. Among this group of believers in Lystra and Iconium, Timothy was well-liked and they spoke favorably of him to Paul. His mother was a Jewish believer, but because of his father's heritage, Timothy was apparently uncircumcised. Because Timothy planned to accompany Paul on his travels ministering to the Jews, he needed to be circumcised. Paul did not consider his circumcision necessary for his salvation, but it was expedient because the Jews would not even consider the words of the apostle if he were traveling with an uncircumcised Gentile.

There is not much said about Timothy's father other than that he was Greek. It is possible that he was dead, but in any case, he doesn't seem to have been part of the picture. It naturally follows, then, that Timothy was raised by his mother and grandmother. And it would also give a new dimension to the close relationship he formed with the apostle Paul later in life.

The next we hear of Lois and Eunice is in 2 Timothy 1, in a letter sent from Paul to Timothy. The apostle says, "I am reminded of your sincere faith, a faith that dwelt first in your grandmother Lois and your mother Eunice and now, I am sure, dwells in you as well" (2 Timothy 1:5). It is clear that Paul held Timothy in high esteem for his devotion and faith in God, and recognized that this faith was first planted by the godly influence of his grandmother Lois and his mother Eunice.

A couple of chapters later, Paul encouraged Timothy to stand firm in the face of persecutions. He says,

> But as for you [Timothy], continue in what you have learned and have firmly believed, knowing from whom you learned it

> and how from childhood you have been acquainted with the sacred writings, which are able to make you wise for salvation through faith in Christ Jesus.
>
> 2 Timothy 3:14–15

Not only had Paul taught Timothy to have courage and remain steadfast, but these convictions had been instilled in him from childhood by his grandmother and mother, Lois and Eunice.

Role in Redemption

So little mention is made of Lois and Eunice in the Scriptures that we are almost tempted to accuse the Bible writers of being negligent. Reading about these two women is like walking by a bakery that has begun operations but has not opened for the day. You sense a wonderful aroma, a delicious promise of tasty delicacies to come, but the doors are locked, and you go on your way with an empty stomach, hungry and daydreaming of pastries.

What we see of Lois and Eunice is as remarkable as it is brief. We expect to see a mother and a grandmother commended for their love, their compassion, their gentleness, their work ethic, or a host of other things. Yet their commendation from Paul revolves around something that we frequently neglect when we speak of the roles of mother and grandmother: theology.

Now, at first you might not see it when you read about Lois and Eunice, but make no mistake, the apostle, who has seen his share of attempted theologians, credits them for being first-rate biblical scholars. Paul reminded Timothy that he knew the Scriptures from childhood. *The Message* puts this in a unique way, saying, "You took in the sacred Scriptures with your mother's milk!" The teachings of the Bible were ingrained in Timothy from birth by two women whom we must conclude were able to teach them because they knew them. Immersion in the Scriptures was not something with which Timothy's family was unacquainted; it was a pastime.

Many families love a particular book, or a series of books. Classics such as *The Pokey Little Puppy, The Chronicles of Narnia, Treasure Island,* and *The Lord of the Rings* may be read over and over again by some families. Those books, however important and valuable they may be, do not require the reader to take action. The test of any theologian, or theology for that matter, is *what does it produce?* A plant that takes in quality sustenance will produce quality fruit; if it does not, there is clearly a problem. The same is true for theology. A theology that does not produce faith is in error. These two women were not merely women who knew the Scriptures, but were women who were remarkable for a faith that was sincere. This faith was noteworthy not just for its presence, but for its quality. Translations differ somewhat on how they translate 2 Timothy 1:5. Some say that this faith "dwelt" in Lois and Eunice while some say that it "lived" in them, and a few even say "filled" them. The point is that this faith was not in a collection of theology books gathering dust on shelves; it was a living, breathing thing.

The world owes these two women a great debt not only because they passed along their faith and a love for God's Word to Timothy, but because they gratefully accepted the role of teacher, and they excelled in it.

By the Numbers

Number of children each woman had (that we know of): 1

Miles between Timothy's hometown of Lystra and Ephesus, his location when he received the letter of 2 Timothy: 266

Things We Wondered

How did Eunice end up married to a Greek if she was a Jewish believer?

Did the apostle Paul also know Lois and Eunice, or did he just hear of them from Timothy?

30

Lydia

The Church Planter

> I half envy Lydia that she should be the leader of the European band; yet I feel right glad that a woman led the van, and that her household followed so closely in the rear.[1]
>
> —Charles Haddon Spurgeon

Scripture References

Acts 16; Philippians 1

Biography

The city of Philippi was the most prominent city of the district of Macedonia, which was a Roman colony. Paul and his team, including Luke, stayed there for a number of days on what is commonly called Paul's second missionary journey. On the Sabbath day, they went outside the city's gates to the riverside, looking for a place of prayer of the Jews. They found a group of women assembled, and so they sat down and began speaking with them. It is possible that there was a synagogue by the riverside, but it is perhaps more probable that Philippi did not have the minimum number of Jewish men (ten) needed to form a synagogue. This dearth of male Jews would explain the location outside the gates, as well as the specific mention of women worshiping.

One of the women who worshiped by the riverside was referred to by Luke in the book of Acts as Lydia.

> Her name, Lydia, may have had some connection with the fact that her hometown stood in an area that was formerly part of the old kingdom of Lydia. Some scholars have even surmised that Lydia was not her name but only her place of origin. We owe coined money to the Lydian kingdom. King Croesus first produced uniform coins there in the sixth century BC. Wealthy King Croesus may have been the person behind the legend of King Midas, whose touch supposedly turned anything to gold.[2]

Whether Lydia was her proper name or a reference to her home region, we do know a few other facts about her as well. She was from the city of Thyatira, she was a seller of purple fabrics, and she was a worshiper of the one true God.

The day that Lydia came into contact with Paul and Luke, God opened her heart to respond to the things spoken by Paul. She and her entire household responded in faith and were baptized. After her conversion, she strongly urged Paul and his companions, "If you have judged me to be faithful to the Lord, come into my house and stay" (Acts 16:15 NASB). They consented to stay at her home, but on the way to her house events transpired (Acts 16:16–39) that led to Paul and Silas's being beaten and imprisoned. After their release, they went to

Lydia's house, saw their fellow believers, encouraged them, and continued on their journey.

Lydia is considered the first European convert to Christianity.

Role in Redemption

She is like a square peg trying to fit into a round hole. He sticks out like a sore thumb. She is the black sheep of the group. He is a fish out of water. She is an odd duck. We have many different (some of them quite odd) idioms and figures of speech for describing people that for one reason or another just do not seem to fit in. Sometimes these people are outcasts, sometimes they are brave trailblazers, and sometimes they are people whom God is setting apart for a particular purpose. Lydia was one such person, although most accurately we might describe her as the purple sheep.

Lydia was a woman who from all appearances ran her own business. It wasn't terribly unusual for a Roman woman to be involved in commerce, but to apparently be the sole proprietor would be highly irregular. She was a Gentile who practiced Judaism. In order to practice her chosen faith she had to go outside of the city. She seems to have had little male oversight in her life, which would have been very unusual for a woman of the day. She freely converses with men, and even invites them to stay at her home, and we get the impression that she might have been a woman of some means. Many of the Bible's most notable women were outsiders, but Lydia seems to have turned being the exception to the rule into an art form.

What is more striking about the story of Lydia, even more than all of the ways in which she ignored or defied conventional societal wisdom, was how intentional God's plan was for her. Notice that everything about who Lydia was comes into play, and then Luke writes, "The Lord opened her heart to respond to Paul's message" (Acts 16:14 NIV). All of the ways in which Lydia had been different were ways in which God had prepared her first to come to faith, and then to fulfill His mission for her. God opened her heart, and she responded by opening her home. Paul and Silas had a brief stay at the home of Lydia, and she continued to be instrumental in the proclamation of the gospel in her city, including the possibility of hosting the church in Philippi.

When the apostle Paul approached a river outside the city of Philippi, he intended to share the gospel with whomever he could find. He found a woman open to being different, and he found a woman whom God had plans for all along. And redemption came to the continent of Europe.

By the Numbers

Specific conversions Luke reported in Acts 16, of which Lydia was one: 3

Miles from Philippi, where the Gangites River was located, the probable location of Paul and Lydia's first meeting: 1.5

Approximate miles from Thyatira, Lydia's hometown, to Philippi: 385

Things We Wondered

Was "Lydia" actually either Euodia or Syntyche mentioned in Philippians 4:2?

How small was the Jewish community in Philippi?

In that culture, how was Lydia free to serve how she wanted to without the typical male supervision?

31

Priscilla

The Apologist

> It is a singular honor which he [the apostle Paul] ascribes here to Prisca and Aquila, especially with regard to a woman. The modesty of the holy man does on this account more clearly shine forth, for he disdained not to have a woman as his associate in the work of the Lord, nor was he ashamed to confess this.[1]
>
> —John Calvin

Scripture References

Acts 18; Romans 16; 1 Corinthians 16; 2 Timothy 4

Biography

Priscilla, along with her husband Aquila, is mentioned six times in four books of the New Testament. The couple is always listed together, never separately. Four times she is mentioned first, and two times he is mentioned first. The name Priscilla is a Roman diminutive form for Prisca, which was her formal Roman name. The two were tentmakers by trade, just as Paul was.

Near the end of Paul's second missionary journey, he came to Corinth. There he came in contact with Aquila and Priscilla, who had left Italy because Emperor Claudius had commanded all the Jews to leave Rome. This expulsion of the Jews from the Roman capital took place around AD 49.

When Paul left Corinth, they left the city and journeyed with him to the city of Ephesus in present-day Turkey. The couple remained in Ephesus while Paul continued his journey back to Antioch. After Paul had left Ephesus, Priscilla and Aquila encountered a man named Apollos. The book of Acts describes Apollos as a man who was "mighty in the Scriptures . . . fervent in spirit." He came to Ephesus proclaiming with boldness in the synagogue in the name of Christ. For all of his gifts and passion, Apollos was lacking in much of the fundamental truth of Christianity. Priscilla and Aquila heard him speak and took him aside to better train and disciple him.

We know little of Priscilla or her husband's life or travels after our introduction to them in Acts 18, but we can roughly sketch together some brief glimpses based on Paul's letters. At the end of 1 Corinthians, Paul makes this statement: "Aquila and Prisca greet you heartily in the Lord, with the church that is in their house" (1 Corinthians 16:19 NASB). We know that 1 Corinthians was written from Ephesus around AD 56, about four years after they arrived in Ephesus with Paul. We can then conclude that for at least four years they were active in the church there, which apparently met in their house.

The epistle to the church in Rome, written within a year or two of his penning 1 Corinthians, includes this nugget by Paul near the end of the book:

> Greet Prisca and Aquila, my fellow workers in Christ Jesus, who for my life risked their own necks, to whom not only do I give thanks, but also all the churches of the Gentiles; also greet the church that is in their house.
>
> Romans 16:3–5 NASB

We can only speculate on the circumstances of their return to Rome, but commentator Douglas Moo suggests the following:

> They apparently served with Paul in Ephesus for some time (1 Cor. 16:19) before returning to Rome after Claudius's edict lapsed. Paul commends Priscilla and Aquila as "fellow workers" (*synergos*), a term he uses regularly to refer to people who minister with him in all kinds of ways (see also vv. 9, 21; 2 Cor. 8:23; Phil. 2:25; 4:3; Col. 4:11; Philem. 1, 24). They have also "risked their lives" for Paul. When this happened we do not know, although it may have been at the time of the riot in Ephesus (Acts 19).[2]

Around a decade later, Paul penned his last written words in the epistle we know as 2 Timothy. Paul wrote this from a Roman prison to his son in the faith, Timothy, who was ministering to the church in Ephesus. At the very end of the book, Paul instructs Timothy to "greet Prisca and Aquila." We know nothing of their reason for having once again moved from Rome to Ephesus. Their faithfulness spanned nearly the entirety of Paul's ministry, and no doubt it continued after he was gone as well.

Role in Redemption

Priscilla is a great woman to be represented in this book's final chapter. In many ways she is exactly what we would hope to see in a Christian woman. Unlike women such as Sarah, Rahab, or Gomer, the Scriptures give us nothing with regard to her faults.

Surely she had them, no doubt Aquila could name a few, but the biblical writers left us nothing with regard to her lesser qualities. We know little about Priscilla, but what we do know tells us that there is much to admire.

First, Priscilla was a *fellow laborer* in every sense of the term: This husband and wife team was a true partnership. Every time we see them in the Bible, they appear together. This dynamic couple comes into contact with the apostle Paul, brings him into their home, and works together, not only in furthering the gospel but also as tentmakers, providing for their own financial needs. Priscilla labored with her husband and the apostle both temporally and spiritually. She and her husband were an ideal duo, and for about a year and a half she was one-third of a team with Aquila and Paul. She was not a spectator. We do not see Priscilla on the outside looking in. She was as involved and industrious as Paul himself.

Second, Priscilla was the dictionary definition of the New Testament concept of hospitality. Hosting large groups is hard work. The size or stature of your house does not matter. Inviting people into your home regularly is hard, often labor-intensive work. As I (Aaron) write this, it is two days until we host the community group that we lead for our church. We host the group twice a month, and I put a lot of effort into seeing that the house is ready for the group, but the effort I put in is dwarfed by how much work my own co-laborer (and coauthor) puts in. She coordinates the food preparations, sees that we have childcare lined up, and, frankly, is far more passionate than I am about making sure the house is clean. With this in the back of my mind, I found my mouth agape as I realized that Aquila and Priscilla hosted the church in Ephesus in their home, and then when they moved back to Rome, they hosted the church there as well. This woman worked a physically demanding job all day, partnered with the apostle Paul in sharing the gospel, and for good measure opened her home as the meeting place for their church in not one, but two different cities.

Third, she was a solid theologian. When Priscilla and Aquila came into contact with Apollos in Acts 18:26, Luke was very specific to note, "*They* took him aside and explained to him the way of God more accurately" (NASB, emphasis ours). Apollos knew the Old Testament backward and forward—he was no theological slouch—but there was much of the life of Christ and the early church that he did not know. Together Priscilla and her husband took him under their wings, counseled him, and discipled him. In a way, it was reminiscent of their dealings with Paul. One can imagine the many deep theological conversations that the apostle and his hosts had while making tents. Now the deep theological conversations resumed, but this time with the host couple as the knowledgeable instructors.

Priscilla was deeply knowledgeable about her faith, and able to clearly communicate it to another person. That was a part of her story, which included escaping a sinful emperor, partnering with an apostle, hosting churches, training teachers, and staying faithful to the end. It makes her a woman whose life was a remarkable story of God's love and redemption.

By the Numbers

References to Priscilla in the New Testament: 6

References to Priscilla in which her husband is also mentioned: 6

Number of times Priscilla is mentioned before her husband: 4

Number of churches that met in Aquila and Priscilla's home over the years: 2

Things We Wondered

Why did Aquila and Priscilla move back to Rome?

How did the couple's discipleship of Apollos work?

What was their marriage like?

Notes

Chapter 1: Eve: The First Woman, the First Sinner

1. John Milton, *Book IX* (911–916).

Chapter 2: Sarah: The Laugher

1. F. F. Bruce, *The Epistle to the Hebrews: The English Text with Introduction, Exposition, and Notes* (U.K.: Marshall, Morgan and Scott, 1964), 300.

2. C. Michael Patton, "Dealing with Doubt," http://www.reclaimingthemind.org/blog/wp-content/uploads/2010/11/Dealing-with-Doubt.pdf. Accessed, January 30, 2017.

3. James R. Slaughter, "Instructions to Christian Wives in 1 Peter 3:1–6," *Bibliotheca Sacra* 153.609 (1996): 63–74. ATLA Religion Database with ATLASerials. Accessed, May 15, 2016.

Chapter 3: Tamar: The Jilted Daughter-in-Law

1. W. G. Plaut, Bernard J. Bamberger, and William W. Hallo, *The Torah: A Modern Commentary* (Union of American Hebrew Congregations, 1981).

2. Derek Kidner, *Genesis: An Introduction and Commentary* (Downers Grove, IL: InterVarsity Press, 1967), 188.

Chapter 4: Jochebed: The Disobedient Slave

1. John Calvin, "Commentary on Exodus 2:4" in *Calvin's Commentary on the Bible*, www.studylight.org/commentaries/cal/exodus-2.html, 1,840–1,857.

Chapter 5: Zipporah: The Wife Who Saved Her Family

1. Tony Evans and Chrystal E. Hurst, *Kingdom Woman: Embracing Your Purpose, Power, and Possibilities* (Carol Stream, IL: Tyndale House, 2013), Internet resource.

2. "The Churchill Society London: Churchill's Speeches." Accessed Web, January 30, 2017.

3. Ronald Barclay Allen, "The 'Bloody Bridegroom' in Exodus 4:24–26," *Bibliotheca Sacra* 153 (1996): 259–269. ATLA Religion Database with ATLASerials. Web, January 10, 2017.

Chapter 6: Rahab: The Abettor

1. William H Willimon, "Best Little Harlot's House in Jericho," *The Christian Century* 100.31 (1983): 956–958. ATLA Religion Database with ATLASerials. Web, January 30, 2017.

2. John Calvin, "Commentary on Joshua," *Christian Classics Ethereal Library*. Accessed Web, January 30, 2017.

Chapter 7: Deborah: The Exceptional Judge

1. Warren W. Wiersbe, *Be Available* (Wheaton, IL: Victor Books, 1994).

2. Sun Tzu, *The Art of War* 9.11, http://classics.mit.edu/Tzu/artwar.html.

Chapter 8: Ruth: The Faithful Foreigner

1. Jonathan Edwards, *Sermons and Discourses*, 1,734–1,738 (WJE online, Vol. 19), ed. M. X. Lesser.

Chapter 9: Naomi: The Bitter Mother-in-Law

1. W. A. Criswell, "The W. A. Criswell Sermon Library." Accessed Web, January 30, 2017.

2. C. S. Lewis, *A Grief Observed* (San Francisco: Harper San Francisco, 2001), 9–10.

Chapter 10: Hannah: The Infertile Woman

1. Tony W. Cartledge, "Hannah Asked, and God Heard," *Review & Expositor* 99.2 (2002): 143–144. ATLA Religion Database with ATLASerials. Accessed, November 14, 2016.

Chapter 11: Bathsheba: The Adulteress

1. Flavius Josephus: *Antiquities of the Jews*, Book VII. 7. http://penelope.uchicago.edu/josephus/ant-7.html.

2. Nathaniel Hawthorne, *The Scarlet Letter* (Champaign, IL: Project Gutenberg, 1990). Internet resource, 154.

3. Alexander Izuchukwu Abasili, "Was It Rape?: The David and Bathsheba Pericope Reexamined," *Vetus Testamentum* 61.1 (2011): 1–15. ATLA Religion Database with ATLASerials. Accessed Web, November 20, 2016, 11.

Chapter 12: The Widow of Zarephath: The Obedient Gentile Widow

1. F. B. Meyer, *Elijah and the Secret of His Power* (Kindle Locations 365–368).

Chapter 13: The Woman of Shunem: The Faithful Hostess

1. Gene Rice, "A Great Woman of Ancient Israel (2 Kings 4:8–37; 8:1–6)." *The Journal of Religious Thought*, 60–63.2–2 (2008): 69–85. ATLA Religion Database with ATLASerials. Accessed Web, November 18, 2016, 79.

Chapter 14: Esther: The Queen

1. Karen H. Jobes, *Esther:The NIV Application Commentary* (Zondervan) (Kindle Locations 668–670).

Chapter 15: Gomer: The Harlot

1. Charles L. Feinberg, *The Minor Prophets* (Chicago: Moody Press, 1976), 24–25.

2. Thomas Constable, *Hosea: Expository Notes*, 2017 edition. http://soniclight.org/constable/notes/pdf/hosea.pdf. Accessed January 30, 2017.

Chapter 16: Mary, Mother of Jesus: Mother of the Messiah

1. Martin Luther and A. T. W. Steinhaeuser, *The Magnificat: Luther's Commentary* (Minneapolis: Augsburg Publishing, 1967).

2. D. R.W. Wood and I. H. Marshall, *New Bible Dictionary* (Leicester, England: InterVarsity Press, 1996).

3. https://www.onfaith.co/discussion/10-things-i-wish-everyone-knew-about-mary-mother-of-jesus.

4. Raymond Edward Brown, "The Annunciation to Mary, the Visitation, and the Magnificat (Luke 1:26–56)." Worship 62.3 (1988): 249–259. ATLA Religion Database with ATLASerials. Accessed, August 31, 2016, 254.

Chapter 17: Elizabeth: The Mother of the Forerunner

1. J. Vernon McGee, *Elisabeth: The First Person to Worship Jesus*. http://articles.ochristian.com/article15674.shtml. Accessed, January 30, 2017.

2. Thomas Constable, *Luke: Expository Notes*. http://soniclight.org/constable/notes/pdf/luke.pdf. Accessed, January 30, 2017.

3. Darrell L. Bock, *Luke: The NIV Application Commentary from Biblical Text to Contemporary Life*, 64 (Zondervan). Kindle edition.

4. Most English translations render the end of Luke 1:59 similarly to the Holman Christian Standard Bible: "They were going to name him Zechariah, after his father." But the verb for *call* is in the imperfect tense, indicating continuous action. Thus, the most likely scenario is that friends and family had already begun to refer to the child as Zechariah in anticipation of the family giving him that name.

Chapter 18: Anna: The Prophetess

1. Matthew Henry, *Matthew Henry's Commentary on the Whole Bible: Complete and Unabridged* (Grand Rapids, MI: Guardian Press, 1976).
2. Josephus, *Antiquities of the Jews* 13.376.
3. Josephus, *Antiquities of the Jews* 14.70–71.

Chapter 19: Mary Magdalene: The Witness

1. D. A. Carson, *The Gospel According to John* (Leicester, England: Inter-Varsity Press, 1991), 636.
2. John Chrysostom, *Homilies on the Gospel of John,* Homily 86, 446–448. http://www.newadvent.org/fathers/240186.htm. Accessed, January 30, 2017.
3. Josephus, *Antiquities of the Jews* 4, 8, 15, trans. H. St. J. Thackeray (New York: Putnam, 1930), 580–581.

Chapter 20: Mary and Martha: The Sisters

1. George Whitefield, *The Care of the Soul Urged as the One Thing Needful.* http://www.biblebb.com/files/whitefield/GW031.htm. Accessed, January 30, 2017.

Chapter 21: The Woman at the Well: The Town Crier

1. R. C. Sproul, *John: St. Andrew's Expositional Commentary*. Kindle Location 859–862.
2. Thomas Constable, *John: Expository Notes.* http://soniclight.org/constable/notes/pdf/john.pdf. 2017 edition. Accessed, January 30, 2017.

Chapter 22: The Bleeding Woman: The Woman Healed by Her Faith

1. Robert H. Gundry, *Commentary on Mark: Commentary on the New Testament Book #2*. Kindle Location 1,266–1,269. (Grand Rapids, MI: Baker Publishing Group.)
2. In Richard Whitekettle, "Levitical Thought and the Female Reproductive Cycle: Wombs, Wellsprings, and the Primeval World." *Vetus Testamentum* 46.3 (1996): 376–391. ATLA Religion Database with ATLASerials. Web, January 25, 2017.
3. Robert H. Gundry, *Commentary on Mark: Commentary on the New Testament, Book 2*. Kindle Location 1,269–1,275 (Grand Rapids, MI: Baker Publishing Group).

Chapter 23: The Syrophoenician Woman: The Believing Beggar

1. J. D. Pentecost and John Danilson, *The Words and Works of Jesus Christ: A Study of the Life of Christ* (Grand Rapids, MI: Zondervan, 1981), 245.

Chapter 24: Widow with Two Mites: The Woman Who Gave All

1. Marjory Clifford, "The Widow's Mite," *The Christian Century* 73.45 (1956): 1287. ATLA Religion Database with ATLASerials. Accessed Web, November 14, 2016.

Chapter 25: The Widow of Nain: The Recipient of Compassion

1. Darrell L. Bock, *Luke: The NIV Application Commentary from Biblical Text to Contemporary Life.* (Grand Rapids, MI: Zondervan). Kindle edition.
2. Craig S. Keener, *The IVP Bible Background Commentary: New Testament* (2014). Internet resource.
3. Carolyn S. Leeb, "The Widow in the Hebrew Bible: Homeless and Post-Menopausal," *Proceedings* (Eastern Great Lakes and Midwest Bible Society) 21 (2001): 61–67. ATLA Religion Database with ATLASerials. Accessed, December 29, 2016.

Chapter 26: The Woman Sinner: The Woman Forgiven of Much

1. Jennifer A. English, "Which Woman?: Reimagining the Woman Who Anoints Jesus in Luke 7:36–50." *Currents in Theology and Mission* 39.6 (2012): 435–441.
2. Craig S. Keener, *The IVP Bible Background Commentary: New Testament* (2014). Internet resource.
3. Alfred Plummer, *A Critical and Exegetical Commentary on the Gospel According to Saint Luke* (Edinburgh: T. & T. Clark, 1922).
4. Darrell L. Bock, *Luke: The NIV Application Commentary from Biblical Text to Contemporary Life* (Grand Rapids, MI: Zondervan). Kindle location, 219.

Chapter 27: Tabitha: The Resurrected Woman

1. Jon M. Walton, "What About Dorcas?" *The Christian Century* 124.8 (2007): 16. ATLA Religion Database with ATLASerials. Accessed, November 13, 2016.
2. Thomas Constable, *Acts: Expository Notes.* http://soniclight.org/constable/notes/pdf/acts.pdf. 2017 edition. Accessed, January 30, 2017.

Chapter 28: Phoebe: The Generous Servant

1. Craig S. Keener, *Romans: A New Covenant Commentary* (Cambridge: Lutterworth Press, 2009). Internet resource, 183.
2. Thomas Constable, *Romans: Expository Notes.* http://soniclight.org/constable/notes/pdf/romans.pdf. 2017 edition, 202. Accessed, January 30, 2017.
3. http://www.ccel.org/1/luther/romans/pref_romans.html.

Chapter 29: Lois and Eunice: The Women of Sincere Faith

1. J. Ligon Duncan III, *A Spirit of Power, Love, and Discipline*. http://www.fpcjackson.org/resource-library/sermons/a-spirit-of-power-love-and-discipline. Accessed, January 30, 2017.

Chapter 30: Lydia: The Church Planter

1. C. H. Spurgeon, *Lydia, the First European Convert*. http://www.spurgeon.org/sermons/2222.php. Metropolitan Tabernacle, Newington, September 20, 1891. Accessed, January 30, 2017.

2. , Thomas Constable, *Acts: Expository Notes*. http://soniclight.org/constable/notes/pdf/acts.pdf. 2017 edition, 231. Accessed, January 30, 2017.

Chapter 31: Priscilla: The Apologist

1. John Calvin and Joseph Haroutunian, *Calvin: Commentaries* (Philadelphia: Westminster Press, 1958).

2. Douglas J. Moo, *Romans: The NIV Application Commentary, Book 6* (Grand Rapids, MI: Zondervan). Kindle locations 10,604–10,609.

Aaron and **Elaina Sharp** are both Master of Theology graduates of Dallas Theological Seminary. Aaron works for Insight for Living Ministries, and Elaina owns and operates a small business.

Aaron is the author of *Everything the Bible Says About Parenting and Children* and *What Does God Say About That?* His writing has been featured in *Discipleship Journal*, *In Touch* magazine, and other Christian periodicals. Elaina writes and develops curriculum for ministries such as Campus Crusade for Christ and others. She has a passion for discipleship and teaching. Aaron and Elaina live in Little Elm, Texas, with their three children.